EUROPA ⚔ MILITARIA Nº8

AIR WAR
OVER THE
GULF

TEXT AND PHOTOS BY

ERIC MICHELETTI

Windrow & Greene

PAY-BACK TIME FOR SADDAM

B aghdad, Iraq; 2.30 a.m. local time, 17 January 1991. In the moonless skies over the capital, an all-black F-117A of the US Air Force — an aircraft at the cutting edge of American technology — approaches its target. The Iraqi defences do not detect the intruder, which is practically invisible to radar. The pilot, from the crack 37th Tactical Fighter Wing, profits from the F-117A's 'stealth' technology to fly over highly defended enemy territory in near immunity from detection. His target is as symbolic as it is highly practical: the ten-floor military telecommunications building of the Iraqi army situated in the heart of Baghdad.

Forty-eight hours ago the period allowed by the United Nations for Saddam Hussein to announce his compliance with the UN resolutions demanding his withdrawal from Kuwait ran out. Now the coalition is ready to take the decision out of his hands.

Approaching his target, the pilot acquires it on the display in his cockpit; and releases a 2000lb BLU-109 bomb. Guided by laser, it steers towards its target. There is a huge explosion, and the building appears to implode under the shock. Six minutes later the Baghdad sky has literally caught fire: hundreds of anti-aircraft batteries blaze away, filling the air over the capital with glowing tracer. But most of them, their target acquisition radars already blinded, are firing wild, and too low to do much damage.

Four waves of aircraft follow that first Stealth raider over Baghdad during the next two hours. The first wave comes from Saudi Arabia, led by F-4G Phantom 'Wild Weasels' to seek out and destroy the Iraqi radars with HARM missiles. In all, 1,400 combat aircraft will take part, of eleven types ranging from the F-117A to the giant B-52. They fly from 30 bases in Saudi Arabia, the United Arab Emirates, Egypt, Turkey, Cyprus, the Indian Ocean, and from six US carriers in the Gulf and the Red Sea, all under the command of USAF Lt. Gen. 'Chuck' Horner.

The carefully targeted 'smart' weapons launched by USAF and US Navy aircraft are followed by Tomahawk cruise missiles fired from US Navy warships on station in the Gulf, the Red Sea and the Mediterranean. With devastating precision the Tomahawks follow the terrain contours across half a country, avoiding natural and man-made obstacles to plunge into their targets with an accuracy measured in a few yards.

As morning breaks the US commanders take stock of the results: single-figure losses, virtually no Iraqi air opposition, and — despite a very large number of triple-A batteries — objectives achieved right across Iraqi territory. Of the 4,000-plus important targets designated in Iraq and occupied Kuwait, all the most critical had been hit on the night of l7 January. The first wave had dropped some 18,000 tons of ordnance. As a US official commented: 'Each of our aircraft can fly two combat sorties a day; in this way, we can drop, each day, the equivalent weight of bombs dropped on Nazi Germany in l5 days at the height of World War II.'

At 8.30 a.m. a second massive raid was launched. The top priority targets were still the enemy's radar installations, communications centres, the runways

4

Above:
Despite the smile, the tension is real for this A-10A Thunderbolt II pilot. In a few minutes he will take off to hunt Iraqi tanks, protected by still-effective 'triple-A'. In 30 days of combat three of these tough, manoeuvrable but necessarily slow ground-attack gun-platforms would be shot down.
(Photo: Yves Debay)

Opposite:
An F-15E Eagle of the 336th TFS, 4th TFW returns from a combat mission; most of its bombs and missiles have been expended — only one AIM-9 Sidewinder remains under the wing.
(Photo: DoD)

of enemy airfields and the hardened concrete shelters protecting his MiGs, various military headquarters, and the symbols of political power — the presidential palace, Saddam's residence, and the headquarters of the Ba'ath Party through which he controlled every aspect of Iraqi life.

While the USAF F-15s, F-16s and F-111s were attacking targets in Baghdad and the central and western regions of Iraq, the F-18s, A-6s and A-7s of the US Navy and US Marine Corps concentrated on the south of the country, where the bulk of the Republican Guard was deployed. B-52s delivered their massive bombloads to Basra, nerve centre of the Iraqi military machine in the Kuwait Theatre of Operations. A third series of raids, again led by the F-117A, hit Baghdad at 7.0 p.m. that evening.

On this first day of the air war just one US Navy F-18 and one Italian Air Force Tornado were reported missing, out of a total of 1,600 sorties: a good omen for the future. The coalition commanders were all too aware of the central importance of a successful air offensive. The timing, nature, and cost of the eventual ground offensive depended upon success in hammering Saddam's forces from above.

There was virtually no air combat. From the first Saddam Hussein, unwilling to send his air assets up to certain destruction, decided to leave his combat jets in their hardened shelters, where he mistakenly believed they would be invulnerable. Thus, allied aircraft had the freedom of the skies over Iraq, and during the days which followed they took out more and more of the enemy's anti-aircraft batteries. In fact their worst problem during the period 18 to 20 January was the bad weather. Many aircraft were

Above:
'Tank-busters' get ready for take-off during the battle for Khafji, late January, to attack columns of T-55s which broke through the Saudi frontier. Several dozen tanks were knocked out by the USAF Thunderbolts.
(Photo: Yves Debay)

forced to return to base with their weapons still on board: in the murky visibility and winter rain it was often impossible for them to 'acquire' targets for their sophisticated ordnance at any altitude, and it was unwise for them to go in low — not only was the flak likely to be deadly, but 'smart' weapons need time and height to operate effectively.

As from 22 January, however, the weather improved and the allied air attacks regained their momentum, in accordance with Gen. Colin Powell's simple and chilling plan for the Iraqi army in Kuwait: 'First we're going to cut it off, then we're going to kill it ...'

At the beginning of the conflict allied aims had been to attack primarily the enemy air defences and the fabric of Iraq's command and control networks. Second came the strategic infrastructure which supported the military — munitions depots, armament factories, and chemical and nuclear facilities above all: the nightmare of Saddam turning to weapons of mass destruction haunted the allies. In the third phase the Iraqi army in the KTO was to be systematically isolated from reinforcement and supply; its 'second echelon' and lines of supply were attacked relentlessly. Taking care not to hit civilian areas, especially in Kuwait, the allies worked through their list of targets.

Twenty days into the offensive, following the destruction of the majority of the Scud launchers — a determining factor in the whole allied operation — and the surprise flight into neutral Iran of more than 100 of Saddam's surviving aircraft (of which ten crashed en route), the allies switched targets again.

Although they continued to fly deep-penetration missions against factories, communication centres, strategic bridges and other choke-points, the majority of the sorties would henceforward be flown against

Top left:
F-16C of the 388th TFW from Hill AFB launches four Mk.82 500-lb bombs. Initially based at Al Mindhat in the UAE, the wing later moved up to Saudi Arabia.
(Photo: DoD)

Below:
Armourers of the 354th TFW load an AGM-65A Maverick ASM under the wing of an A-10A.
(Photo: Yves Debay)

Above:
A B-52G strategic bomber rains a stick of parachute-retarded bombs over the desert. At the height of the air war formations of three to five B-52s attacked Iraqi military targets in Kuwait every three hours.
(Photo: DoD)

tactical targets: the Iraqi army's large tank formations, strong artillery, troop concentrations and support units. By 17 February the Pentagon estimated that 600-700 tanks had been destroyed, as well as 650 artillery pieces and 600 other armoured vehicles. Out of an estimated total of 300,000 tons of Iraqi munitions stockpiled in Kuwait some 40,000 tons had been destroyed.Allied pilots, flying solo or in pairs, ranged over the desert in a 'free hunt' for

Above: **A formation of tank-killers, the nearest with a single Maverick ASM left on a starboard wing strongpoint. The heavily-armoured A-10 was designed around the 30mm rotary cannon, whose depleted uranium round penetrates most tanks.** *(Photo: USAF)*

This A-10A pilot has kept his older-style flying helmet — for luck? *(Photo: DoD)*

USAF UNITS IN THE GULF

Aircraft types	Units & bases (all Saudi Arabia unless otherwise stated)
Air superiority fighters 120 F-15C/D Eagle	1st TFW Dhahran, 33rd & 36th TFW Tabuk
Fighter-bombers 192 F-16C/D Fighting Falcon	50th TFW Tabuk, 363rd TFW Al Dhafra, 388th TFW Al Mindhat (UAE), 401st TFW Diyarbakir
Bombers 48 F-15E Eagle 14 F-111E Aardvark 50 F-111F Aardvark 36 F-117A Nighthawk	4th TFW Thumrayt (Sultanate of Oman) 20th TFW Incirlik (Turkey) 48th TFW Taif 37th TFW Khamis Mushayt
Long-range bombers 45 B-52G Stratofortress	42nd & 93rd BW Diego Garcia, 92nd BW Moron (Spain), Fairford (UK).
Attack aircraft 114 A-10A Thunderbolt II 10 AC-130H Spectre	10th TFW Hafar al Batin, 23rd TFW Tabuk 354th TFW Al Jubayl 1st SOW Riyadh
Electronic warfare 42 F-4E/G Phantom II 12 EF-111A Raven 4 EC-130H Hercules	35th and 52nd TFW, Muharraq (Bahrain) 366th TFW Taif 552 AW&CW Hafar al Batin
Reconnaissance and AEW 18 RF-4C Phantom II 4 TR-1A/U-2R 7 E-3A/C Sentry 3 RC-135U/V/W Stratolifter	117th TRW Riyadh 9th SRW Akrotiri (Cyprus) 552nd AW&CW Riyadh 55th SRW Riyadh
Battlefield reconnaissance 18 OA-10A Thunderbolt II	602nd TACW Hafar at Batin
Transport and flight refuelling 110 C-130E/H Hercules 8 MC/HC-130E/N Hercules 60 KC-135E/R Stratotanker	Bases in Saudi Arabia and UAE 1st SOW Riyadh 1701st ARW Riyadh/Jeddah

suitable targets. Only small-calibre triple-A rose to meet them: the SAM batteries had been silenced.

At this point the number of allied air sorties flown each day rose to about 2,800. Basra, the strategic centre of the theatre, was effectively cut off from the capital. Charred tanks began to litter the Kuwaiti desert. The main road between Baghdad and Kuwait City was reduced to some ten per cent of normal traffic capacity. One Iraqi source hinted at 20,000 military fatalities and three times that number of wounded. Front-line troops on the Kuwait border were reduced to a handful of rice a day, and even water was short. In a textbook operation, the huge allied air offensive had combined technological sophistication, sound strategy and psychological insight to reduce the enemy's ground forces to a condition which only the final lightning advance of 24-28 February would fully reveal. ❒

F-15C EAGLE

The F-15C Eagles of the 1st Tactical Fighter Wing arrived at Dhahran air force base as early as mid-August 1990, and provided vital air cover for the allied build-up during Operation 'Desert Shield'.
(Photo: Eric Micheletti)

Right:
F-15C of the 1st TFW searing up from a Saudi air base under the thrust of its Pratt & Whitney F-100
(Photo: Eric Micheletti)

AIR SUPERIORITY FIGHTER

McDONNELL DOUGLAS F-I5C EAGLE

Crew: One
Top speed: 1,680mph
Powerplant: Two Pratt & Whitney F-100 PW-100
Basic weight: 12.8 tons
Loaded weight: 19.7 tons
Length: 63.6ft.
Height: 18. ft.
Wing span: 42.6 ft.
Armaments: 1 x M61A1 20mm rotary cannon, 4 x AIM-7F Sparrow & 4 x AIM-9L Sidewinder AAMs
Variant: F-15E low-altitude all-weather strike/attack variant with IR capability

Opposite top:
Impressive view of the F-15E Eagle in the markings of the wing commander of the 4th Tactical Fighter Wing, based at Thumrayt, Oman.
(Photo: DoD)

Opposite bottom left:
Insignia of the F15-equipped units in the Gulf. *Top to bottom and left to right:* **1st TFW, 27th TFS, 71st TFS; 33rd TFW, 58th TFS, 60th TFS; 36th TFW, 22nd TFS, 53rd TFS, 525th TFS. 53rd TFS, 525th TFS.** *(Houssais Collection)*

Opposite bottom, right:
Ground crew preparing an F-15C for a combat sorie. On 17 January at 3.15a.m. one of the F-15s escorting the first raids over Baghdad, piloted by Capt. Steve Tate, destroyed a Mirage F-1 with an AIM-7F Sparrow missile. *(Photo: Eric Micheletti)*

8

9

SELECTION OF TARGETS

The precise bombing of so many strategic targets from the first hours of the air war made it clear that potential objectives had been identified long beforehand. The invasion of Kuwait in August 1990 started the CIA, DIA and NSA on an intensive hunt for information to flesh out existing contingency planning. Agents sought useful information initially in Europe, Korea and Pakistan, from construction companies who had helped build military and strategic facilities. A picture was built up of the materials and construction methods, the layouts, and even the location of certain critical equipment. Contact with Eastern intelligence agencies also proved fruitful. The images and recorded radio traffic provided by a range of reconnaissance satellites were of the greatest value, identifying command and control centres in particular. US agencies thus gathered detail on several thousand targets, which they were able to collate into a practical catalogue of targets for the armed forces. ❏

Left:
At Dhahran air base armourers of the 1st TFW make a final check on AIM-9L Sidewinder air-to-air missiles. Note the Sparrow missiles, still without their warheads. *(Photo: Yves Debay)*

Below:
An everyday sight on the Saudi bases: a USAF technician ducks into the air intake of an F-15C to check the condition of the compressor blades. *(Photo: Eric Micheletti)*

Above:
Rear taxiing view of one of the 1st TFW's F-15Cs leaving a hardened shelter at Dhahran. Carrying three drop-tanks, it will be able to roam at will in Iraqi skies literally emptied of all air opposition. The Eagles never had a real chance to pit themselves against the best Iraqi interceptors or pilots. *(Photo: Eric Micheletti)*

Above right:
In the best traditions of the USAF, this captain's F-15C is personalised with 'nose art' — a cherished survival even in these days of hazy grey camouflage and minimal markings. *(Photo: Eric Micheletti)*

Right:
Insignia of units flying the F-15E, F-111E and F-111F.
Left, top to bottom:
4th TFW, 335th TFS, 336th TFS (F-15E); 79th TFS (F-111E).
Centre:
20th TFW, 55th TFS, 77th TFS (F-111E).
Right:
48th TFW, 492nd TFS, 493rd TFS, 494th and 495th TFS (F-111F).
(Houssais Collection)

THE KILLING ZONES

From the second week of the air offensive the allied pilots divided the battlefield, especially in Kuwait, into numbered squares termed 'killing zones'. Sector by sector, the fighter-bombers were vectored onto specific targets, clearing each zone. They were supported by ECM aircraft, which comprehensively jammed Iraqi radars; and tankers cruising at high altitude to refuel incoming and returning missions. This whole deadly aerial ballet was meticulously choreographed by the AWACS.

The extraordinary 'Star Wars' outline of an F-117A
Nighthawk of the 37th Tactical Fighter Wing, the first
unit to hit Baghdad on the night of 17 January 1991.
(Photo: DoD)

F-117A NIGHT- HAWK

On the night of l7 January, at 2.20 a.m. local time, the F-117A Nighthawks of the two squadrons of the 37th Tactical Fighter Wing — the famous 'Stealth fighters' — penetrated Iraqi airspace. Without causing the least echo on Iraqi radar screens they navigated the moonless skies towards their targets: the most strategically vital buildings and sites in and around Baghdad, which had to be knocked out in the first minutes of the shooting war to blind and deafen the enemy's immediate retaliatory capacity.

The city was still brightly lit-up as the black bat-shapes whispered in for the kill. Destruction lanced down out of the skies without the least warning, and with the almost uncanny precision of laser-guided bombs. While the Iraqis were still reacting with noisy but blind fury, the first Tomahawk cruise missiles began to arrive with equal precision and devastating effect.

The success of the F-117A in the Gulf has silenced various media wiseacres who drew the wrong lessons from its combat debut during the US operations against Panama a year previously. Its performance in the opening hours of Operation 'Desert Storm' was far more indicative of its true capability.

On the night of l7 January the Nighthawks were targeted against — among other strategic sites — the main military telecommunications centre and the Iraqi aviation ministry headquarters, both of which were destroyed with laser-guided bombs.

The first F-117As had arrived in Saudi Arabia in mid-August l990 with the initial deployments under Operation 'Desert Shield'. Between that date and January 1991 unit strengths in-theatre were built up until, on the eve of the first combat missions, the USAF had 36 F-117As from the two squadrons of the 37th Tactical Fighter Wing stationed at Khamis Mushayt in Saudi Arabia.

As the air war progressed the types of missions with which the unit was tasked began to widen. From the initial communications centres and command-and-control facilities, the Nighthawk's prey began to include missile launch sites and storage areas; the factories manufacturing and maintaining the long-range Scud missiles of Scud-B, Al-Abbas and Al-Hussein variants, whose potential threat both to allied military bases and concentrations and to civilian targets in Saudi Arabia and Israel was a major political consideration in the middle weeks of the air war, particularly in view of the then-rumoured Iraqi chemical capability; and finally the plants producing Saddam Hussein's chemical weapons, and his remote nuclear research and production plant.

The F-117A is an astonishing step forward in aircraft design: a combat aircraft which is for all practical purposes invisible to enemy radar by virtue

Right: top to bottom:
Insignia of the 37th Tactical Fighter Wing, and its two squadrons: 416th TFS 'Grim Reapers', and 415th TFS, 'Nightstalkers'.

F-117A refuelling in flight from a KC-10 tanker —
the contrast between these two generations of
aircraft is almost surreal. On combat missions over
Iraq the Stealth aircraft could carry out this
manoeuvre in total darkness.
(Photo: DoD)

of its outline, materials and finish. It is, logically
enough, allocated the best-defended and most high-
value targets. Its 'invisibility' allows it to penetrate
the most modern and effective radar air defence
networks undetected and unintercepted. The
Nighthawk can thus attack at higher altitudes than
classic fighter-bombers, which have to fly 'under the
radar' to avoid detection; and it thus has more time
to acquire its target.

It has a radius of action of some 1,100 miles, and its
weapons bay can carry up to 4,000lbs. of bombs and
missiles. Its navigation and attack system is designed
to give the pilot full autonomy while maintaining
radio silence; and it can be refuelled in flight in
conditions of complete darkness. The navigation
and attack system features an INAS with Forward-
Looking-Infra-Red and Downward-Looking-Infra Red
sensors, coupled with a laser designator. This permits
the aircraft to 'illuminate' the target from weapon
launch until the moment of impact. Normally a single target will be assigned to two F-117As, the second
only attacking if the first run should fail for any
reason.

For 'Desert Storm' American commanders re-
served the Nighthawk's amazing capabilities for
targets of high value where extreme precision was
required — typically, targets no more than 300 ft. in
length or width; and also to fixed targets deep inside
Iraq and defended by particularly effective anti-aircraft sites. That the F-117As accomplished these
difficult missions with a 90 per cent success rate and
without any loss to themselves speaks volumes for
this new American weapons system. ❑

F-117A pilots are
selected from the elite of
the USAF. *(Photo: DoD)*

LOCKHEAD F-117A FIGHTER-BOMBER

Crew: One
Top speed: Subsonic (c.550 mph)
Powerplant: Two General Electric F-404
Basic weight: classified
Loaded weight: classified
Length: 25.9 ft.
Height: 14 ft
Wing Span: 44.9 ft.
Armament: Up to 4,000 lbs. warload in weapons bay

Two Stealth fighters on a Californian air force base:
once again, from whatever angle they are viewed the
F-117As look more like products of the imagination of
George Lucas' SFX wizards than in-service USAF
combat equipment. *(Photo: DoD)*

B-52G

Top:

B-52Gs of the 92nd Bombardment Wing lined up on a Spanish air base. From the first week of February a dozen of these super-heavy bombers would be flying missions from Europe against the Iraqi army.

The pilot's fist controls the brute power of the B-52's eight mighty engines. *(Photos: USAF)*

At the centre of events in a war in which the extraordinary capabilities of 'smart' weapons have been demonstrated in full for the first time, the B-52 — veteran of the Vietnam War of more than 20 years ago — continued to play an important role. The massive load-carrying capacity and the sheer intimidating size of this SAC battlewagon produce both destructive results and a powerful psychological impact.

From the start of 'Desert Shield' in August 1990 some 30 B-52Gs from the 69th Bombardment Squadron, 42nd Bombardment Wing based at Loring AFB, Maine, and the 328th BS, 93rd BW from Castle AFB, California were deployed to the island of Diego Garcia in the Indian Ocean. These Stratofortresses started combat operations on the night of 17 January 1991, dropping 13 tons of high explosive on armament factories in central Iraq.

From then on, both by day and by night, formations of from two to five B-52Gs continued to hit Iraqi targets. From the second week of the air war they extended their targets from strategic sites to include the Iraqi army's rear echelons. The third week saw a slight change in targeting, with the B-52s' baleful attention drawn to Iraqi mechanised units moving up to the Saudi frontier. Saddam's vain aim at this stage seems to have been to provoke the coalition ground commanders into a premature land campaign.

Comparison with the American bombing campaign over Vietnam is inevitable. The B-52 is perhaps best remembered for the concerted raids of the 'Linebacker II' operation, which involved formations of five aircraft hitting a single target in a staggered series of attacks; these raids terrorised the North Vietnamese troops. Comparisons are largely meaningless, however, given the evolution of Strategic Air Command bombing tactics since the late 1970s. Blind bombing from high altitude is out: nowadays, says a senior SAC officer, 'we utilise the B-52 to the full, making use of its long range, its low-altitude precision bombing capability, and its defensive ECM systems.'

The B-52G, despite its apparent age, is in fact a modern weapons system; thanks to regular avionics up-dates, only the basic airframe and the eight engines remain from the days of Vietnam. It has been progressively modernised right up to 1989, and the Offensive Avionics System (OAS) up-date in 1987 marked a particularly important step forward in overall capability. Sixty-nine of the B-52Gs in the SAC inventory received a terrain-following radar identical to that used in the Tomahawk cruise missile. A defensive electronic countermeasures (ECM) suite is capable of handling 16 enemy radars, and of jamming 12 of them simultaneously. Two pods are fitted under the nose: one contains a low-light TV camera, the other an FLIR — the ALQ-172 Pave Mint, developed by ITT Avionics. In the rear of the aircraft is installed a radar system capable of detecting when the bomber is being 'painted' by an enemy radar —

The USAF's Strategic Air command has nine Bombardment Wings flying the B-52G — a total of 163 aircraft. These bombers have received numerous avionics 'up-dates' including several to the defensive ECM suite; the B-52G is today capable of carrying out low-level penetration missions, as flown regularly over Kuwait against Iraqi mechanised units. *(Photo: USAF)*

The insignia of the Strategic Air Command.

Below:
From 5 February 1991 onward the B-52Gs intensified their night operations against the rear echelons of the Iraqi army, and later hit the front-line positions in Kuwait, typically flying one mission every three hours. A huge tonnage of bombs was dropped and immense damage was done both to Iraqi material and to the morale of the front-line troops. *(Photo: USAF)*

either from an interceptor or a missile — and launching chaff or flares for self-defence.

Alongside these avionics up-grades came a modernisation of the aircraft's offensive armament. The B-52 is capable of carrying a panoply of ordnance ranging from the classic Mk.82 500lb. 'iron bomb' (27 of them in the bomb bay and 24 more on underwing strongpoints) to the new AGM-142A Have Nap air-surface missile and the AGM-88 HARM anti-radar missile. This latter is a new development for the B-52; in 1988 Gen. John Chain, commander of the SAC, declared: 'With this anti-radar missile the B-52 becomes even more independent; it can now fire ahead, 'blinding' its target so that it can bomb without danger from ground-based defences.' Several B-52Gs of the 328th Bombardment Squadron used these HARM missiles during the first few days of operation 'Desert Storm'.

During the last week of January the American commanders decided to increase the strategic bombing capability by sending aircraft of the 92nd Bombardment Wing to bases in western Europe. In the United Kingdom the bombers deployed to RAF Fairford north-west of London, which has one of the longest runways in Europe. From Fairford (where the USAF personnel were welcomed back, particularly by the pub-keepers of the village near the 'moth-balled' base!) the B-52Gs flew bombing missions over southern Iraq and occupied Kuwait, their route taking them right across France and the Mediterranean Sea. In Spain the B-52Gs landed at Moron-de-la-Frontera near Seville early in February. To keep up the supply of bombs (60 tons a day) Spanish air force C-130 Hercules transports made three shuttle flights daily between Zaragoza and Moron.

On 2 February a B-52 of the 93rd Bombardment Wing was lost over the Indian Ocean. On the same date the targeting was changed for the remainder; their new mission was to obliterate the large-scale land defences — sand berms, extensive minefields, supporting bunkers and trench complexes, artillery positions, dug-in armour, and the stockpiled material for the garrison divisions — which Saddam's army had constructed and manned all along the Kuwaiti coastline and inland along the borders of Kuwait and Saudi Arabia. With a dreadful regularity, every three hours, the SAC bombers released their iron thunder over Iraqi garrisons with devastating effect: the enemy's true losses will never be known, but the ineffectual resistance offered to the eventual allied ground thrust speaks for itself.

Despite its age the B-52G remains the only suitable type for high-altitude strategic bombing in the USAF inventory. (The new B-1B, its intended successor, was not deployed to the Gulf, probably both because of technical problems with its engines and to avoid the risk of losing such an expensive aircraft.) One B-52 can drop a greater weight of explosive on its target than can five fighter-bombers, or a salvo from a battleship. For Iraqi conscripts and Republican Guards, as for Vietnamese *Bo-Dois*, the B-52 remains the terror of the skies. ❐

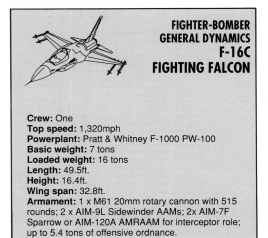

Left:
Before climbing into his cockpit an F-16 pilot of the 388th Tactical Fighter Wing carries out a last-minute check of his armament, including this AIM-9L Sidewinder. *(Photo: USAF)*

F-16 FIGHTING FALCON

FIGHTER-BOMBER GENERAL DYNAMICS F-16C FIGHTING FALCON

Crew: One
Top speed: 1,320mph
Powerplant: Pratt & Whitney F-1000 PW-100
Basic weight: 7 tons
Loaded weight: 16 tons
Length: 49.5ft.
Height: 16.4ft.
Wing span: 32.8ft.
Armament: 1 x M61 20mm rotary cannon with 515 rounds; 2 x AIM-9L Sidewinder AAMs; 2x AIM-7F Sparrow or AIM-120A AMRAAM for interceptor role; up to 5.4 tons of offensive ordnance.

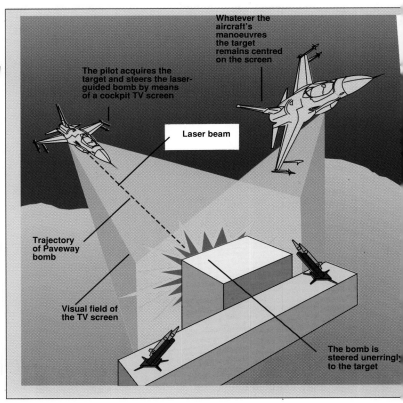

The pilot acquires the target and steers the laser-guided bomb by means of a cockpit TV screen

Whatever the aircraft's manoeuvres the target remains centred on the screen

Laser beam

Trajectory of Paveway bomb

Visual field of the TV screen

The bomb is steered unerringly to the target

Left:
With undercarriage down and all ordnance removed (probably after maintenance), an F-16C of the 10th TFS, 50th TFW normally based at Hahn, Germany. During the Gulf war the 50th TFW operated from Tabuk, flying many missions against Iraqi targets of opportunity in the first half of February. *(Photo: DoD)*

Right:
The insignia of the F-16 units deployed to the Gulf.
Left column:
363rd TFW, and its 17th TFS, 33rd TFS; 50th TFW.
Centre:
388th TFW, and its 34th TFS, 421st TFS; 10th TFS of 50th TFW.
Right:
401st TFW, and its 612th TFS, 613th RFS, 614th TFS.
(Houssais Collection)

'PAVEWAY' SYSTEM

he 'Paveway' family of weapons is duced by Texas Instruments, and prises six types of bomb, all laser-ed. The four main types are desig-d GBU-10E/B, Mk.13/18, GBU-/B, and GBU-12D/B.

eveloped from a conventional 'iron b', the Paveway is fitted with an isition system in the nose. Once bomb is launched this equipment ives the signal from a laser designa-fitted to the aircraft (Pave Knife, Tack, Atlis, Lantirn, etc), allowing omb to be steered by means of its ns. In the Pave Tack system a video era holds the target centred on a TV en in the cockpit regardless of any oeuvres made by the launching air-.

elatively inexpensive and simple to truct, the Paveway system is em-ed by many of the world's air forces. likely that some pin-point raids on targets were laser-designated by ial Forces teams in-country. ❏

(Diagram: J.M. Mongin)

Right:
Back from a sortie, and before taking a break until the briefing for his next mission, an F-16 pilot writes up the inevitable log book.
(Photo: DoD)

17

F-111

By the time night fell over the desert on 16 January 1991, the United States Air Force had 60 F-111E/F long range strike/attack fighter-bombers in the Gulf theatre. The 'Aardvarks' belonged to the 48th Tactical Fighter Wing, stationed at Taif, Saudi Arabia; and the 20th TFW, whose F-111Es were detached to Incirlik in Turkey, with ten at RAF Akrotiri in Cyprus. Operating with them were twelve EF-111A Ravens from the 366th TFW, also at Taif, whose role was to protect the strike force by comprehensive jamming of enemy radar and communications. The F-111s and EF-111s took part in the huge allied attack formation which pounded Iraq and occupied Kuwait from 2.30a.m. on 17 January, in the first hour of the air war.

STRIKE/ATTACK AIRCRAFT

GENERAL DYNAMICS F-111F

Crew: Two
Top speed: 1,680mph
Powerplant: Two Pratt & Whitney TF 30
Basic weight: 21.5 tons
Loaded weight: 45.3 tons
Length: 73.5ft.
Height: 17ft.
Wing span, swept: 31.1ft. **Unswept:** 62.9ft.
Armament: Weapons bay accomodates 14 tons of ordnance or M61A1 20mm rotary canon; 4 x external strongpoints carry 9-plus tons.
Variants: F-111A, D, E, all-weather strike/attack, FB-111 strategic bomber, EF-111 electronic warfare

Providing the electronic jamming capability for its formation, an EF-111A Raven from the 366th TFW keeps its distance from the rest of the attacking aircraft. During the first few days of the war the Ravens 'blinded' the acquisition radars of the Iraqi 'triple-A' and SAM batteries.
(Photo: USAF)

Flying with the F-15Es, surrounded by EF-111As and RF-4Cs, and preceded by the F-4Gs, the F-111s rained their laser-guided munitions on to more than a hundred major enemy targets that night - strategic sites of all types, command-and-control facilities, ground-based air defences, and airfield runways. The results were impressive, both in the precision achieved and in the miraculously low level of allied losses: neither F-111 Wing suffered a single casualty on this raid. It was a faultless performance by the highly professional and long-trained aircrews; and Saddam Hussein discovered the hard way — just as had Colonel Gaddafi, in his time — the terrible efficiency of the F-111. As one of the pilots said: 'We've been here five months; now we're doing what we were sent here to do - and doing it well.'

Above:
An F-111F from the 48th TFW based at Lakenheath, England, bombs at medium altitude with parachute-retarded munitions. With a range of 3,000 miles, the 'Aardvark' can carry 24 x 750lb. bombs on four underwing pylons. *(Photo: USAF)*

Right:
Just before take-off everything looks good to this F-111 navigator. Enemy defences were plentiful but not generally accurate, and the F-111s enjoyed the freedom of Iraq's skies by day and night. *(Photo: USAF)*

THE ATTACK CORRIDOR

Diagram of a typical mission for a USAF EF-111A — the aircraft at top left, with an electronic countermeasures pod on top of its tail fin. The role of the EF-111A is to create a corridor of electronic jamming down which the F-111F fighter-bombers can pass unhindered through Iraqi airspace without being picked up by the acquisition radars of SAM batteries. The Ravens employ their comprehensive ECM suite (ten jamming transmitters) to complement the more limited ECM fit on the other allied fighter-bombers.

(Diagram: J. M. Mongin)

F-4G 'WILD WEASEL'

Above:
Although it is now more than 30 years old, the Phantom still has a role to play as a specialised defence-suppression and electronics countermeasures aircraft. Here HARM anti-radar missiles are loaded on to the first F-4G Wild Weasels on the night of 16 January, when even the technicians on the ground did not know the exact destination of their aircraft.
(Photo: DoD)

ELECTRONIC WARFARE AIRCRAFT

McDONNELL DOUGLAS F-4G WILD WEASEL

Crew: Two
Top speed: 1,500mph
Powerplant: Two General Electric J79-GE-17
Basic weight: 14 tons
Loaded weight: 27.5 tons
Length: 63ft.
Wing span: 38.4ft.
Height: 16.25ft.
Wing span: 38.4ft.
Armament: 2 x AIM-7F Sparrow, 4 x AIM-9L Sidewinder, 2 x AGM-45 Shrike; plus 2 x AGM-76 ARM, or 2 x AGM-88 HARM, or 6 x AGM-65 Maverick

Above:
Paired missions have long been practised in Central Europe, as by this F-4G from Spangdahlem, Germany, turning in tight formation with its 'guardian angel', an F-16C armed with Sidewinder and Sparrow missiles.
(Photo: USAF)

Right:
The evening of the first day of the air war: F-4Gs refuel in flight, returning yet again to sniff out and destroy the last few surviving Iraqi radar systems.
(Photo: DoD)

Right:
Insignia of USAF close air support units deployed to the Gulf. *Top to bottom, left to right:* **1st Special Operations Wing** (AC-130H Spectre II); **10th Tactical Fighter Wing, 511th Tactical Fighter Squadron; 23rd TFW, 74th & 76th TFS; 354th TFW, 33rd & 356th TFS** (all A-10A Thunderbolt II).

Below:
Badges of USAF electronic warfare units deployed to the Gulf. *Top to bottom, left to right:* **35th TFW, 561st TFS; 81st TFS** (unofficial); **52nd TFW, 23rd, 81st & 480th TFS** (all F-4G Wild Weasel); **366th TFW, 390th ECS** (EF-111A Raven); **552nd AW&CW, 41st ECS** (EC-130H).

Below right:
602nd Tactical Air Control Wing, 23rd Tactical Air Support Squadron, both equipped with the OA-10A Thunderbolt II forward observation and control variant. *(All photos courtesy Houssais Collection)*

US AIR FORCE SPECIALISED UNITS

A-10A

Above:
Preparing to take off from A1 Jubayl, an A-10A from the 23rd TFW carries underwing AGM-65A Maverick missiles. Named officially in honour of the tank-busting exploits of the old World War II Republic P-47 Thunderbolt, it is popularly known as the 'Warthog' for its extravagant ugliness. The pilots of this extraordinarily manoeuvrable ground-attack craft love it anyway: it accounted for hundreds of Iraqi tanks.

Left:
The A-10A was designed around massive armour protection from the inevitable storm of ground fire it faces, and a deadly 30mm rotary cannon with 1,100 rounds 'in the clip'. Here it sports the snarling fangs so beloved of any American fighter jock who can get away with it, since the days of the 1940s Air Volunteer Group in China. *(Photos: Yves Debay)*

CLOSE SUPPORT AIRCRAFT
FAIRCHILD REPUBLIC
A-10A THUNDERBOLT

Crew: One
Top speed: 440mph
Powerplant: Two General electric TF 34 100
Basic weight: 11.3 tons
Loaded weight: 22.7 tons
Length: 53.4ft.
Height: 14.6ft.
Wing span: 57.4ft.
Armament: 1 x 30mm general Electric GAU-8/A Avenger rotary cannon, max. rate of fire 4,200rpm, plus up to 7 tons of ordnance on 11 external pylons.
Variants: 0A-10-A version for battlefield observation

AC-130 SPECTRE

Above:
Three-quarter view of an AC-130 from the 919th Special Operations Squadron based at Eglin AFB, Florida. The Spectres did massive execution over the Iraqi front lines in Kuwait.
(Photo: USAF)

The concept of the multi-engine transport modified to mount heavy side-firing 'broadsides' of ground-attack guns was born in Vietnam, with the AC-47 — 'Puff the Magic Dragon'. The Hercules battlewagon is a fearsomely effective up-dating of the concept; although obviously vulnerable to massed or sophisticated anti-aircraft defences, in the right environment they offer the ground troops tremendous firepower in pin-point support. Their large crews can handle a varied battery of weapons; their size and range allow a great deal of ammunition to be carried, and a long 'loiter' time over the target. The AC-130 was blooded in Vietnam, and subsequently used successfully in Grenada and Panama. It was an obvious choice for Gulf service; and the USAF sent ten AC-130H Spectre IIs from the 1st Special Operations Wing at Hurlburt Field, and others from the Air Force Reserve, out east immediately after the Iraqi invasion of Kuwait.

The installed armament includes a 105mm cannon, a 40mm, and two 20mm rotary cannon (in the AC-130V these latter being replaced by a single 25mm weapon). As effective by night as by day, the Spectre pin-points its target and maintains its aim by means of infra-red and video cameras; then circles in a 30 degree bank, pouring a concentrated stream of fire out of the sky. The 20mm guns have a rate of fire of 3,000 rpm; the 40mm, 1,000rpm; and the 105mm, ten rounds a minute.

One AC-130 was lost over Kuwait early in February, apparently on a secret mission in support of US Special Forces operating deep inside enemy territory. (The wreck was subsequently located off the coast close to the Saudi border.) ❐

Left:
Gun crewmen round the mounting of a 40mm cannon in the hull of an AC-130. The firepower of the Spectre is so great that crewmen have to carry snow-shovels on missions, so that they can clear the great drifts of expended cases from around the gun-mountings.
(Photo USAF)

23

THE US NAVY SHOWS ITS MUSCLES

From the start of the crisis in August 1990 the United States was determined to ensure its complete air superiority over the Gulf. Six attack carriers were deployed to the area, followed in February 1991 by a seventh; and these patrolled both the Gulf and the Red Sea. This huge armada, unequalled since the Pacific War, allowed the US Navy to bring to bear 50 combat squadrons. When the air war opened these squadrons, alongside USAF and US Marine Corps units and the air contingents of other coalition countries, quickly achieved not only air superiority but air supremacy. They were then free to apply some of their resources to helping destroy Iraqi factories, strategic sites and all kinds of military targets.

The US high command stationed the USS *Midway* and USS *Ranger* in the Gulf area while the USS *John F. Kennedy*, USS *America* and USS *Saratoga* cruised in the Red Sea. The sixth carrier, USS *Theodore Rossevelt*, did not employ its aircraft operationally during the first days of the war; its A-6 Intruders and F/A-18 Hornets joined the fray after a week and a half.

During the night of 16/17 January the five US carriers launched many waves of fighter-bombers, interceptors and ECM aircraft. Those from the Red Sea passed right across the skies of the Arabian peninsula to dive on targets in western Iraq before refuelling in flight for the long return to their floating bases.

For the squadrons launched from the flight-decks of the carriers patrolling the eastern coasts the distance was shorter, but their missions took them deep into Iraqi airspace. There was no shortage of targets: there were literally hundreds of them, listed

Above:
An A-7E Corsair II from CVW-3, embarked on the USS *John F. Kennedy.* **In service since 1966, the LTV Corsair II had its hour of glory in Vietnam; but 20 aircraft of this type were still to fly on successful combat operations over Iraq.**
(Photo: Yves Debay)

in books as thick as telephone directories.

After two days of combat operations the losses were exceptionally low: only one A-6 and one Hornet had failed to return from their missions. At the same time the seventh carrier, USS *Forrestal*, sailed into the Mediterranean to patrol off the coast of Israel.

While the ground-attack types — the A-6 Intruder, A-7 Corsair II and F/A-18 Hornet — pursued their work of destruction, F-14A Tomcats were tasked with providing air defence against enemy strikes on the carrier groups. But Iraqi aerial activity was almost non-existant, and the combat air patrols lessened in importance. The same situation obtained throughout

24

Above: **Intense activity on the flight-deck of the USS** *John. F. Kennedy;* **24 hours a day, the F-14A Tomcats of CVW-3 provided combat air patrols over the carrier groups, and escort cover for the Navy attack types heading for Iraq.**

Left: **Hook and flaps down, an A-6E Intruder of CVW-8 on the final approach to the USS** *Theodore Roosevelt's* **welcoming flight-deck; its bomb pylons are empty... An up-graded model of an old design, the Intruder carried out the majority of US Navy bombing missions alongside the F/A-18 Hornet.**

(Photos: Yves Debay)

Iraqi skies from 1 February, when the allies — though cautious in case of surprises — almost grudgingly accepted that they had achieved total air supremacy. Those few Iraqi combat jets which had come up to fight had been shot down in short order; those which survived the raids on their airfields, and could still take off, were apparently intent only on fleeing for sanctuary in neutral Iran. The Tomcats were virtually out of work...

The Gulf operations gave the US Navy a unique opportunity to test new weapons under operational conditions, however. This was particularly welcome in the case of the SLAM (Stand-Off Land Attack Missile), equipping Intruders and Hornets, which was still under development. The SLAM is a high-performance, high-precision weapon developed from the Harpoon, and can be launched from very low altitude.

Left:
Corsair and Intruder pilots head for their aircraft and another mission. The first month of the air war cost the US navy some ten aircraft lost in combat.
(Photo: Yves Debay)

US NAVY AIRCRAFT IN THE GULF

Aircraft type	Air Wings, with ship or shore base
Air superiority fighter 100 x F-14A Tomcat	USS *America* (CVW-1), *Ranger* (CVW-2) *J.F. Kennedy* (CVW-3), *T. Roosevelt* (CVW-8), *Saratoga* (CVW-17)
Fighter-bombers 90 x F/A-18 Hornet 20 x A-7E Corsair II	USS *Midway* (CVW-5), *America* (CVW-1), *T. Roosevelt* (CVW-8), *Saratoga* (CVW-17) USS *J.F. Kennedy* (CVW-3)
Bombers 126 x A-6E Intruder	USS *America* (CVW-1), *Ranger* (CVW-2), *J.F. Kennedy* (CVW-3), *Midway* (CVW-5), *T. Roosevelt* (CVW-8)
Electronic warfare 30 x EA-6B Prowler	USS *America* (CVW-1), *Ranger* (CVW-2), *J.F. Kennedy* (CVW-3), *Midway* (CVW-5), *T. Roosevelt* (CVW-8)
Airborne early warning 30 x E-2C Hawkeye	USS *America* (CVW-1), *Ranger* (CVW-2), *J.F. Kennedy* (CVW-3), *Midway* (CVW-5), *T. Roosevelt* (CVW-8), *Saratoga* (CVW-17)
Anti-submarine warfare 40 x S-3B Viking 8 x P-3C Orion	USS *Ranger* (CVW-2), *J.F. Kennedy* (CVW-3), *T. Roosevelt* (CVW-8), *Saratoga* (CVW-17) FAW-2: Masirah, Oman
Transport & refuelling 3 x KC-130P Hercules 3 x C-9B Skytrain	 VR-22: Muharraq, Bahrain VR-55: Al Jubayl & Tabuk, Saudi Arabia

F-18
HORNET

Above & right:
With its outer wing panels still folded, this F/A-18
Hornet from CVW-17 aboard the USS *Saratoga* taxies
towards one of the catapults. These versatile aircraft
carried out more than 60 per cent of the bombing
missions over Iraq. The flight-deck crews aboard the
US Navy's carriers got not a moment's rest, as each
aircraft flew at least two sorties every day.
(Photos: Yves Debay)

Above:
The Air Wings of the US carriers on station in the Red Sea concentrated on the western area of Iraq, seeking out military targets of opportunity but especially the elusive mobile Scud launchers.
Above right:
Tensed to absorb the acceleration of a catapult launch, an F/A-18 pilot gets ready to deliver 7 tons of ordnance to Iraqi targets. *(Photos: Yves Debay)*

Right:
Insignia of US Navy and US Marine Corps fighter-bomber units. *Top row:* VA-46 (Corsair II, USS *J.F. Kennedy*), VFA-15 (Hornet, USS *T. Roosevelt*), VFA-25 (Hornet, USS *America*). *Second row:* VA-72 (Corsair II, USS *J.F. Kennedy*), VFA-87 (Hornet, USS *T. Roosevelt*), VFA-151 (Hornet, USS *Midway*). *Third row:* VMFA-235, VMFA-451, VMFA-333; *bottom*, VMFA-314 — all US Marine Hornet units based at Muharraq, Bahrain.
(Houssais Collection)

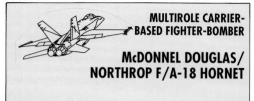

MULTIROLE CARRIER-BASED FIGHTER-BOMBER

McDONNEL DOUGLAS/ NORTHROP F/A-18 HORNET

Crew: One
Top speed: 1,190mph
Powerplant: Two general Electric F-404-400
Basic weight: 9.3 tons
Loaded weight: 22.7 tons
Length: 55.7ft.
Height: 15ft.
Wing span: 40.3ft.
Armament: 1 x M61A1 20mm rotary cannon (570 rounds), 7.5 tons of ordnance on 9 external pylons
Variants: CF-18 land-based for Canadian Forces, RF-18 reconnaissance.

Above:
Formation of Hornets from VFA-113, embarked on the USS *America*. The F-18 in the foreground carries two 500-lb. Mk.82 'iron bombs', and a single drop-tank on the ventral pylon. *(Photo: US Navy)*

Right:
An F-18 pilot on a mission over Saudi Arabia. On the first day of the air offensive one Hornet flying from the USS *Saratoga* was downed by an Iraqi SAM; but losses over the whole six-week war have been extremely light. *(Photo: DoD)*

Left:
F-18s on the flight-deck of the USS *America*. In the foreground, a Hornet of VFA-25 in air superiority configuration; beyond, an aircraft of VFA-113 in the fighter-bomber role. Flight refuelling by USN KC-130s allowed the F-18s to carry out many deep penetration raids over Iraq. *(Photo: US Navy)*

Above:
Final approach by an A-7E Corsair II of CVW-3 embarked on the USS *John F. Kennedy*. **This aircraft has clearly loosed off all its ordnance over Iraqi targets.** *(Photo: Yves Debay)*

Left:
Readying the *JFK's* Corsairs for another mission; in the foreground, an AGM-88A HARM anti-radar missile. *(Photo: DoD)*

Below:
A brief moment of respite for the Corsair pilots between missions. **The 20 Corsairs of VA-46 and VA-72 sent to the Gulf will surely be the last A-7s to see combat, after an active Navy career of more than twenty years.** *(Photo: Yves Debay)*

A-7E
CORSAIR II

F-14 TOMCAT

Above:
24 hours a day, the decks of the six US Navy carriers in the Gulf, the Red Sea and the Mediterranean resounded to the roar of catapult launches. This Tomcat prepares to launch from USS *Saratoga* in the Red Sea, to escort Corsairs tasked with bombing Iraqi artillery batteries. *(Photos: Yves Debay).*

Right:
For 48 hours, from the second day of the air war, weather conditions in the Gulf were bad; but missions continued nonetheless. *(Photo: DoD).*

Opposite:
US Navy Tomcats from VF-41 on the flight-deck of USS *Theodore Roosevelt* in Gulf waters. The best air superiority fighter in the world faced little aerial opposition during its thousands of combat missions over Iraq and occupied Kuwait. *(Photos: Yves Debay).*

Above:
A Tomcat lifts off from the USS *Theodore Roosevelt* for a night interdiction mission; his chances of finding 'trade' are slim... *(Photo: Yves Debay)*
Right:
The badges of most of the F-14 units deployed to the Gulf theatre — only VF-2 'Bounty Hunters' from USS *Ranger* is missing. *Top to bottom, left to right:* VF-14 'Top Hatters' (USS *John F. Kennedy*), VF-102 'Diamondbacks' (USS *America*), VF-74 'Bedevillers' (USS *Saratoga*); VF-32 'Swordsmen' (USS *John F. Kennedy*), VF-233 'Starfighters' (USS *America*), VF-103 'Sluggers' (USS *Saratoga*); VF-1 'Wolfpack' (USS *Ranger*), VF-41 'Black Aces' (USS *Theodore Roosevelt*), VF-84 'Jolly Rogers' (USS *Theodore Roosevelt*). *(Houssais Collection)*

AIR SUPERIORITY FIGHTER

GRUMMAN F-14 TOMCAT

Crew: Two
Top speed: 1,590mph
Powerplant: Two Pratt & Whitney F-110 GE-400 turbofans
Basic weight: 18.1 tons
Length: 62.6ft.
Height: 16ft.
Wing span: swept 38ft., unswept 63.9ft.
Armament: 1 x M61A1 20mm rotary cannon; 6 x AIM-54C Phoenix long-range AAMs; 4 x AIM-7F Sparrow and 2 x AIM-9L Sidewinder AAMs; 6 x AIM-120 AMRAAM

An A-6E from the USS *Saratoga*. The Intruder still provides the US Navy's basic long-range strike capability. *(Photo: Yves Debay)*
Below:
An A-6E over the desert, loaded for bear with 12 Mk.36 bombs, an AGM-88 ASM and an LAU-3/A rocket pod. *(Photo: DoD)*

A-6E INTRUDER

Below:
An Intruder landing on the *Midway*. The A-6E proved capable of withstanding heavy Iraqi 'triple-A'.
(Photo: Yves Debay)

TACTICAL STRIKE AIRCRAFT

GRUMMAN A-6E INTRUDER

Crew: Two
Top speed: 645mph
Powerplant: Two Pratt & Whitney J52-P-8B
Basic weight: 12.1 tons
Loaded weight: 27.4 tons
Length: 54.7ft.
Height: 16ft.
Wing span: 52.8ft.
Armament: according to mission, 4 x Harpoon ASMs; 12 x Mk.36 mines; 30 x Mk.82 500-lb bombs; 4 x Paveway II bombs; one B43 nuclear weapon.

There was little difference between the blue of Arabian skies and those over El Toro, California, home base of the F/A-18 Hornets of VMFA-314. The twelve fighter-bombers of this unit took off every day from Muharraq, Bahrain, to bomb Iraq. *(Photo: Yves Debay)*

US MARINE CORPS AIR ASSETS IN THE GULF

Opposite, bottom:
At low altitude, and armed to the teeth with Mk.84 bombs, an AV-8B Harrier of VMA-331 skims the desert from its base at Al Jubayl.
(Photo: DoD)

From the start of the air war the US Marine Corps' air assets were committed to intense operations against Iraqi units. Initially the 'flying Leathernecks' were tasked with missions against the enemy front line along the Kuwaiti border. Whenever Iraqi artillery opened up on USMC positions, OV-10 Bronco spotters brought Marine AV-8B Harrier II 'jump-jets' or F/A-18 Hornets quickly to the scene to destroy the enemy's revealed batteries. This type of operation is not without its risks, however: about ten aircraft were lost, mostly to small calibre anti-aircraft fire.

Although it was not much discussed at the time, the USMC had some 300 combat aircraft and heli-

copters in theatre to support the 40,000 Marine troops in the Gulf and Red Sea. This considerable air force was under the command of Maj. Gen. J. Moore; its assets were drawn from the 2nd Marine Air Wing, Fleet Marine Force Atlantic, and the 3rd MAW, Fleet Marine Force Pacific.

It was a balanced force, capable of independent action. US Marine headquarters deployed its own air defence in the shape of the 48 F-18 Hornets brought from bases at Kaneohe Bay in Hawaii, El Toro in California, and Beaufort, South Carolina. With them came 12 long-range A-6E strike aircraft belonging to VMA-224. Two squadrons of KC-130 tankers flight-refuelled Marine aircraft during long

Above:
The crew of an OV-10 Bronco of VMO-2 at the A1 Jubayl base on the Saudi coast. The 24 Broncos deployed by the USMC kept up permanent observation of the battlefield on the Kuwaiti frontier north of Marine ground units. *(Photo: Yves Debay)*

missions. For close air support the 1st Marine Expeditionary Force deployed its 36 AV-8B Harrier II vertical/short take-off fighter-bombers. The Marines are the only US service to operate this British aircraft, and they proved their worth yet again during the battle for Khafji in late January. Although the USMC took most of their aircraft ashore, ten Harriers of VMA-223 remained embarked aboard USS *Saipan* in case of amphibious operations against the Kuwaiti coast. ❏

US MARINE AIR UNITS IN THE GULF

Fighter-bombers		
48 x F-18A Hornet	VMFA-235	Muharraq
	VMFA-314	Muharraq
	VMFA-333	Muharraq
	VMFA-451	Muharraq
Bombers		
12 x A-6E Intruder	VMA-224	Muharraq
Close support		
36 x AV-8B Harrier II	VMA-311	Al Jubayl
	VMA-331	Al Jubayl
	VMA-542	Al Jubayl
Electronic warfare		
12 x EA-6B Prowler	VMAQ-2	Muharraq
Observation		
24 x 0V-10A Bronco	VMO-1	Al Jubayl
	VMO-2	Al Jubayl
Refuelling		
24 x KC-130 Hercules	VMGR-252	Muharraq
	VMGR-352	Muharraq

AV-8B HARRIER

TACTICAL SUPPORT AIRCRAFT
McDONNELL DOUGLAS AV-8B HARRIER II

Crew: One
Top speed: 740mph
Powerplant: One Rolls-Royce Pegasus F402-RR-406
Basic weight: 6.6 tons
Loaded weight: 13.5 tons
Length: 46.2ft
Height: 11.8ft
Wing span: 30.1ft
Armament: 1 x GAU-12/U 25mm rotary cannon; seven pylons carrying AIM-9L Sidewinder AAMs and various offensive stores

Above: AV-8B of VMA-311, whose home base is Yuma, Arizona. Still the world's only operational vertical take-off and landing combat aircraft, the British-designed Hawker Harrier is ideal for the USMC's battlefield close support needs, especially in a beachhead where ground facilities may be rudimentary. *(Photo: Eric Micheletti) Above right:* Night falls, but this AV-8B is ready to go at a moment's notice, with two 600-lb. bombs. *(Photo: DoD) Below:* One of twelve Harriers of VMA-311, photographed at Al Jubayl only a few minutes' flying time from Kuwait. They helped stop the Iraqi push at Khafji stone dead in late January 1991. *(Photo: Eric Micheletti)*

OV-10 BRONCO

Above:
An OV-10A and (right) an OV-10B, its long nose containing a laser designator. Both serve with VMO-2 at Al Jubayl. *(Photo: Yves Debay)*

Right:
Rear view of an OV-10A of VMO-2, showing the unusual twin-boom layout. Half these aircraft received a desert paint scheme on arrival in the Gulf from their base at MCAS Cherry Point, South Carolina. *(Photo: Eric Micheletti)*

Below right:
Line-up of VMO-2's OV-10A and OV-10B Broncos. Their low stalling speed makes them ideal battlefield observation aircraft; their mission is hazardous, however, and two were lost. *(Photo: Eric Micheletti)*

TACTICAL RECONNAISSANCE AIRCRAFT
ROCKWELL INTERNATIONAL OV-10A BRONCO

Crew: Two
Top speed: 290mph
Powerplant: Two Garrett T-76-G-420 turboprops
Basic weight: 4.5 tons
Loaded weight: 6.5 tons
Length: 41.3 ft
Height: 15.1ft
Wing span: 40ft
Armament: 4 x podded 7.62mm machine guns, plus 3,600lbs. of external offensive stores

THE FRENCH AIR FORCE CONTINGENT

Wednesday 16 January, 9.00p.m.: from the White House, President Bush telephones President Mitterand in Paris. 'H-Hour' has been confirmed. The French air force's role in the first attacks has been agreed: French aircraft will take part in the second wave of raids at dawn on the 17th. Orders are passed via the chief-of-staff, General Schmitt.

At 5.30a.m. local time, Iraq has been under attack for some three hours. Twelve of the 24 French Jaguar fighter-bombers of the 11th *Escadre de Chasse* take off from their base at A1 Ahsa south of Dhahran. Their target is the Iraqi air base at Ahmed-al-Jabar, 18 miles south of Kuwait City. As well as neutralising the ground-to-air missile batteries and airfield communications, the Jaguars are also tasked with attacking a Scud missile store. They are given top cover by USAF F-16Cs; and their path is prepared by F-4G Wild Weasels to suppress enemy radar. The

Above:
In the early morning light on the taxiway of Al Ahsa air base a Mirage F-1CR of the 33rd *Escadre* rolls out for a combat mission. *(Photo: SIRPA-Air)*

Left:
The pilot of a Mirage 2000RDI adjusts his G-suit before a four-hour combat air patrol. *(Photo: SIRPA-Air)*

Right:
Jaguar A of the 11th *Escadre de Chasse* refuels in flight; it is equipped with a Barax jamming pod, and four 500lb. SAMP bombs. *(Photo: SIRPA-Air)*

HIGH SPEED BOOM

THE FRENCH AIR FORCE IN THE GULF

(Combat units only)

12 x Mirage 2000RDI	5th Escadre de Chasse	**Al Ahsa**
8 x Mirage F-1C	12th Escadre de Chasse	**Doha**
24 x Jaguar A	11th Escadre de Chasse	**Al Ahsa**
4 x Mirage F-1CR	33rd Escadre de Chasse	**Al Ahsa**

Not a still from 'The Right Stuff', but a French air force mechanic carrying out last-minute checks on a Mirage F-1CR of the 33rd *Escadre*. It carries two 500-lb. bombs, two Matra R550 Magic AAMs, a Matra Phimat chaff dispenser on the left pylon, and an ECM jamming pod.
(Photo: SIRPA-Air)

Jaguars are armed with 500-lb. bombs, Belouga cluster bombs, and with laser-guided AS-30L missiles. They will operate at very low altitude.

The F-4Gs successfully knocked out the enemy radars and communication sites using AGM-45 Shrike and AGM-88 HARM munitions; no heavy SAMs were fired during the raid, but the 'triple-A' was intense, as over all Iraqi airfields. One of the Jaguar pilots described his six minutes over Kuwait as follows:

'Half an hour after leaving the runway, in pairs and heavily loaded, we crossed the Kuwait frontier. Already lines of tracer were coming up towards us, and in the distance I noticed a refinery belching huge clouds of black smoke. We were approaching the target at an altitude of 150 feet, while the US fighters kept watch above us. The triple-A was suddenly all around us; 23mm ZSU cannon and SAM-7 light missiles had been massed all round the airfield. Strangely, over the target itself there was a moment of relative calm. At last, ahead of us, we saw the buildings which housed the Iraqi missiles.

'The first AS-30 left the aircraft, and detonated. There was no time to enjoy the spectacle. To relieve my tension I opened up with my 30mm cannon. That's a bit less weight to carry home… Behind me the other guys released their cluster bombs over the runways: what a firework display! Finally, everyone was clear of the target area, and we set course for base. I looked at my watch and found we had been over Kuwait for just six minutes.'

In this baptism of fire four of the French Jaguars had been damaged. Two of these took hits in the engine, and were forced to land at the American air base at Al Jubayl. A third was hit in the cockpit canopy and the pilot was slightly wounded. The first debriefing of the war proved most instructive for the conduct of future operations.

The next day, 18 January, at 5.00a.m. twelve Jaguars again took off in flights of four and headed for Kuwait. This time their target was a large munitions depot of the Iraqi army at Ras-al-Quilayah, south of Kuwait City. A thousand yards long and 750 yards wide, it comprised hangars and protective concrete walls, some of them placed to protect stocks of Exocet MM-39 sea-skimming missiles captured in August 1990 from the Kuwait navy - a weapon which exercised the minds of allied naval commanders considerably.

The two waves of Jaguars flew without top cover, and attacked at medium altitude, profiting from the earlier destruction of Iraqi radars and SAM target acquisition systems. The Jaguars carried a mix of war-loads: either four 500-lb. bombs, or two Belougas, or, on four aircraft, a single AS-30L balanced by a 260-gallon drop-tank under the other wing. The French aircraft dropped their bombs in a dive, and fired their AS-30L missiles from 5,000 yards. Twenty-four hours later the same Jaguars would fly the mission again, to complete their success.

Although the Jaguars received the lion's share of press coverage, the Mirage 2000RDI was also represented in each day's operations. As the first Jaguar

Left:
Insignia of the 5th *Escadre de Chasse* **from Orange, southern France.** *Centre,* **the** *Escadre* **badge, with from left to right** *escadrilles* **SPA 124 and 26 of** *escadron* **1/5** *Vendée,* **and** *escadron* **2/5** *Ile-de-France.*
(Houssais Collection)

Above:
Mirage F-1CR pilots of the 33rd *Escadre* shortly after returning from a mission over Kuwait. *(Photo: SIRPA-Air)*

Below:
Mirage 2000RDI of the 5th *Escadre* on the tarmac at Al Ahsa. *(Photo: Eric Micheletti)*

raid went in on 17 January six Mirage 2000s from the 5th *Escadre de Chasse* were patrolling Saudi skies on air defence duty, in co-ordination with the other allied air superiority fighters. Similar missions were flown on the days which followed; the Mirages were armed with Matra 530D and Magic 2 missiles, and flew four-hour sorties, refuelled in flight by five C-135FRs based at Riyadh.

From Sunday 20 January the bad weather over the whole Gulf region forced a marked slow-down in the level of allied air operations, and the fourth Jaguar mission was disrupted by storms. While modern aircraft are designed for all-weather operations the

pilot still has to be able to see his target if he is to use his laser-guided weapons effectively - even the smartest of 'smart' munitions have their limitations. Poor meteorological conditions also affect the aircraft's electronic systems, which are vulnerable to the electromagnetic discharges of a storm. Finally, a carefully planned sequence of operations requires accurate visual data on the effectiveness of each raid; and while close reconnaissance, even direct overflights in the face of heavy anti-aircraft fire, are part of the job, it is pointless risking pilots and aircraft if the murky ceiling blinds eyes and cameras alike.

AIR SUPERIORITY FIGHTER

DASSAULT-BREGUET MIRAGE 2000C

Crew: One
Top speed: 1,460mph
Powerplant: SNECMA M53-P2
Basic weight: 7.5 tons
Loaded weight: 17 tons
Length: 47.1ft
Height: 17ft
Wing span: 29.9ft
Armament: 2 x DEFA 554 30mm cannon (250 rounds); external war-load of 6.3 tons
Variants: 2000B two-seater; 2000N two-seat tactical nuclear bomber

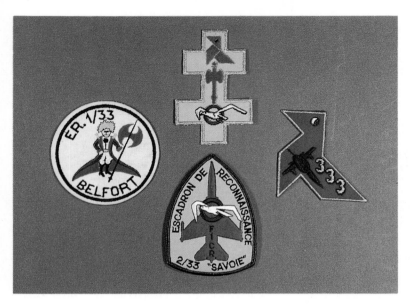

ing warships and installations as well as anti-aircraft defences.

The Jaguars had by now developed a well-established combat routine. The degraded state of the enemy's ground defences allowed them to avoid small-calibre fire by bombing from 15,000 feet.

From Thursday 24 January the political ambiguity which had shadowed French military operations in the Gulf was resolved, and restrictions were removed. On that day a wave of Jaguars and escorting Mirage 2000s carried out two raids inside Iraq for the first time. In future French aircraft carried out daily bombing sorties, the majority on targets in Iraq.

After this first week of the air war several senior French officers began to regret that the Mirage 2000N — which was night-capable — had not been sent to the Gulf. The French Tactical Air Forces had 75 of these high-performance all-weather aircraft available; but a political decision had been taken not to commit a nuclear-capable aircraft to the theatre.

The second week of operations was marked by the entry into operations of five Mirage F-1CRs of the 33rd *Escadre de Reconnaissance*. Although deployed to the Gulf since autumn 1990 they had not yet been committed to combat, since Iraq too had Mirage F-1s and the risk of mistaken identity in the heat of a sortie was felt to be too great. However, the almost complete absence of Iraqi aircraft from the sky reduced this risk to an acceptable level; and on the morning of 26 January two co-ordinated raids were carried out by Jaguars and Mirage F-1CRs on the logistic echelons of Republican Guard units astride the Iraq-Kuwait border. Forty-eight hours later the same aircraft made two further raids on the command centres of the Guard.

By the end of the third week the allied command considered that 80 per cent of Iraqi anti-aircraft assets and more than 30 per cent of the Iraqi army's equipment in the theatre had been destroyed by coalition air action. During this period the French had flown 200 missions, all without loss. ❐

Above:
Insignia of the 33rd *Escadre:* **top centre, the** *escadre,* **and from left to right** *escadrons* **1/33** *Belfort,* **2/33** *Savoie* **and 3/33** *Moselle.*
(Houssais Collection)

On Wednesday 23 January the Jaguar raids began again. This time the major target was the large naval base south of Kuwait City. This operation was flown in conjunction with American, British and Italian aircraft. The Mirage 2000, seen for the first time over Kuwait, provided top cover at 30,000ft.

The Iraqi defences were not in a position to put up much resistance. Only three SAM batteries now remained operational, out of 50 on the eve of the allied air offensive (ten batteries of SA-2, 15 of SA-3 and 25 of SA-6). On several occasions allied jets were 'illuminated' by target acquisition radars, and the tell-tale buzzer sounded in the pilots' ears; but the enemy SAM batteries soon switched their radar off so as not to reveal themselves to the deadly HARMs. They had too little equipment left to take risks with it. The naval base was effectively attacked, destroy-

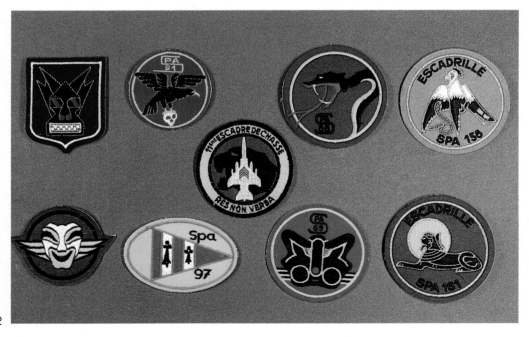

Left:
Insignia of the 11th *Escadre* **from Toul. Centre, the** *escadre;* **left to right, in vertical pairs, the** *escadrilles* **of** *escadrons* **1/11** *Roussillon,* **2/11** *Vosges,* **3/11** *Corse* **and 4/11** *Jura.*
(Houssais Collection)

Above:
Returning from a strike against the Iraqi Republican Guard, this Jaguar A of the 11th *Escadre* **has empty under-wing pylons.** *(Photo: SIRPA-Air)*

Right:
Puma of helicopter *escadron* **1/67** *Pyrénées* **ready for a rescue mission on the tarmac at Al Ahsa.** *(Photo: SIRPA-Air)*

PUMA RESCUE HELICOPTERS

At the Al Ahsa air base nobody took much notice of the two Pumas parked at some distance from the Jaguars, Mirage F-1CRs and 2000s. These humble choppers belonged to COTAM, the French military transport command; and had the mission of search and rescue for pilots downed either in 'friendly' desert or behind enemy lines. While several US aircrew were rescued by USAF ARRS helicopters during the first weeks of 'Desert Storm', the French combat pilots mercifully suffered no losses. In early February, however, one of the French Pumas was tasked to recover a US Navy pilot shot down in a heavily-defended part of Kuwait. After approaching over the coast the Puma — handsomely escorted by A-10 Thunderbolts at low altitude and F-15s above — located and picked up the pilot and returned him safely to Al Jubayl.

JAGUAR

With up-rated armament, the 23-year-old Anglo-French Jaguar fighter-bomber did yeoman service in the Gulf. One handicap — perhaps overstressed by the media — was its inability to take part in night attacks during the early stages of the air offensive.

Night attacks, to be sufficiently precise, need an adequate navigational system: an inertial platform which, once fed with the co-ordinates of the target before the mission, continuously plots the position of the aircraft and displays the waypoints, correcting errors of track en route. The French Jaguars of the 11th *Escadre* had nothing to compare with the Ferranti 1064-INF inertial navigation system fitted to the Royal Air Force's Jaguar GR.1s, enabling their British counterparts to take part in night missions.

The French Jaguar's lack of night capability is no reflection on the basic airframe, which is excellent; it is rather the result of a lack of defence funding — a situation not unique to France. Many other allied aircraft types committed to 'Desert Storm' operated under the same restriction, including the USAF's F-16A and A-10A and the elderly Kuwaiti A-4 Skyhawks.

A muscular fighter-bomber, with 12 underwing pylons capable of carrying up to 4.5 tons of weaponry, the Jaguar justified its nicknames of 'bomb-truck' and 'wheelbarrow bomber'. Flight-refuellable, and capable of carrying a wide range of bomb and missile munitions, the Jaguar had already made its mark over other deserts — those of Mauritania and Chad — well before the Gulf conflict. ❐

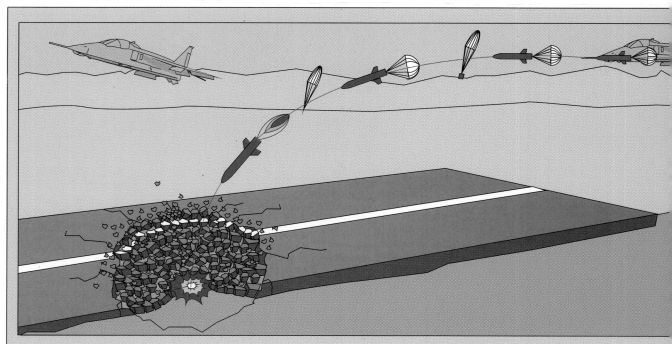

TACTICAL FIGHTER-BOMBER
DASSAULT-BREGUET JAGUAR A

Crew: One
Top speed: 1055 mph
Powerplant: Two Rolls-Royce/Turbomeca Adour
Basic weight: 7 tons
Loaded weight: I5.7 tons
Length: 55.2ft. **Height:** 16 ft.
Wingspan: 28.5ft.
Armament: 2 x 30mm DEFA 553 cannon (300
rounds), plus range of bombs, AS-3OL ASM, Matra
AS-37 Martel, etc.

Below:
**Several hours before an early morning mission the
ground crew load 500-lb. bombs onto the pylons of
Jaguars; these men were the unsung heroes of the war.**
(Photo: SIRPA-Air)

DURANDAL, THE RUNWAY-BUSTER

e Durandal is a specialised runway-attack mis-
roduced by Matra and unique in the Western
al. Apart from the French Air Force, which
t successfully against Iraqi airfields, the USAF
dered 8,500 Durandals, (half the total produc-
for its F-4, F-15E, F-16 and F-111 aircraft.
idal can be launched at altitudes as low as 300
l at speeds of 600-plus mph. After launch a
ig parachute opens. As soon as the missile
es the optimal angle of 30° the parachute is
ned and a rocket motor fires, driving the war-
lown at the 800 ft./second needed to penetrate
hes of concrete before exploding. Time-delay
ation can also be selected.
ram: J.M. Mongin)

A pair of Mirage F-1CRs patrol over Saudi Arabia. Operating alongside the Jaguar A 'bomb trucks', this multi-role reconnaissance fighter with a modern navigation system contributed greatly to the accuracy of attacks. Serviceability in the Gulf was good — better, in fact, than on French home bases. *(Photo: SIRPA-Air)*

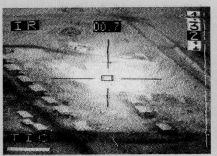
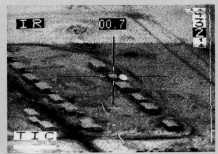

MIRAGE F-1CR

Left:
**Frozen moments from
different bombing raids
made with the French
AS-30L laser-guided
missile. The targets are
various hangars in
occupied Kuwait holding
captured stocks of
Exocet sea-skimming
missiles.**
(Photos: SIRPA-Air)

Above right:
**Mirage F-1CR pilot
returning to Al Ahsa
base after a combat
sortie.** *(Photo: SIRPA-Air)*

The always aggressive export sales programme of the Dassault company had counted Iraq among its successes. The prospect of French and Iraqi Mirage F-1CRs sharing skies full of hungry US fighter jets was not enticing: the repercussions if a French aircraft had been shot down by coalition interceptors would have been considerable… During the first week of combat in the air, the Mirage F-1CR was not committed to operations.

On 26 January, however, in the light of the almost total lack of Iraqi air opposition, this order was rescinded. Combined raids by Mirages and Jaguars were authorised, giving the *Armée de l'Air* an extra string to their tactical bow. The numbers involved were insignificant — of the eight F-1CRs which had arrived in September 1990 three had since returned to their home base at Strasbourg and one had been damaged in a training accident. However, the four available aircraft of the 33rd *Escadre* were valuable for reconnaissance missions, the role for which the unit is primarily trained.

With a complete modern avionics fit the Mirage F-1CR (C for *'chasse'*, 'fighter', and R for reconnaissance) carries Omera 33 cameras, for vertical photography at medium altitude; Omera 40s for horizon-to-horizon photography; and a Super-Cyclone infra-red detection system to identify targets at night.

For ground-attack missions the F-1CR can be equipped with an identical range of offensive armament to that carried by the Jaguar: 'iron bombs', runway-cratering BAP-100, BAT-120 tactical bombs, and the Belouga cluster system. It is a superb all-round multi-role fighter, with a modern navigation system, and it gave the Jaguars great assistance during raids on Iraqi ground positions. ❐

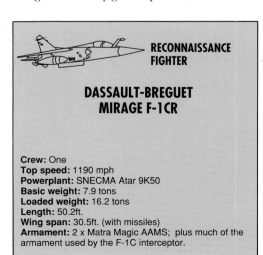

**RECONNAISSANCE
FIGHTER**

**DASSAULT-BREGUET
MIRAGE F-1CR**

Crew: One
Top speed: 1190 mph
Powerplant: SNECMA Atar 9K50
Basic weight: 7.9 tons
Loaded weight: 16.2 tons
Length: 50.2ft.
Wing span: 30.5ft. (with missiles)
Armament: 2 x Matra Magic AAMS; plus much of the armament used by the F-1C interceptor.

JAGUAR AND AS-30L

T he war in the Gulf proved the value of the combination of the Jaguar fighter-bomber and the Aerospatiale AS-30L missile. Despite its age, and its daytime-only navigation system, the Jaguar is an excellent launch-platform for tactical weapons. This proved especially true of the AS-30L in combination with the Thomson-CSF Atlis laser designator pod.

The AS-30L has been in service with the *Armée de l'Air* since 1986. It is a supersonic missile with a solid fuel motor, using laser guidance, and designed for

Left:
Mission accomplished, a Jaguar pilot is questioned about the 'triple-A' over the target by his lieutenant-colonel. *(Photo: SIRPA-Air)*

THE BELOUGA

Designed and built by Matra, this is a parachute-retarded dispenser weapon which distributes 151 x 66mm, 2.8-lb sub-munitions during a single pass over the target. At the moment of firing the pilot can choose either to lay a long strip (about 800ft. by 130ft., or 100,000 sq.ft. area), or a pattern about 400ft. in each direction (about 50,000 sq.ft.) depending upon the target. The munitions approach the target nearly vertically for maximum damage. Three types of munitions are available: fragmentation, which can pierce 4mm of steel at 30ft.; anti-tank, which can penetrate 25mm of sheet steel; and area denial — like the fragmentation but with delayed fusing. The Belouga is just over 10ft. long, weighing 670lb. of which 430lb. are the sub-munitions.

(Diagram: J. M. Mongin)

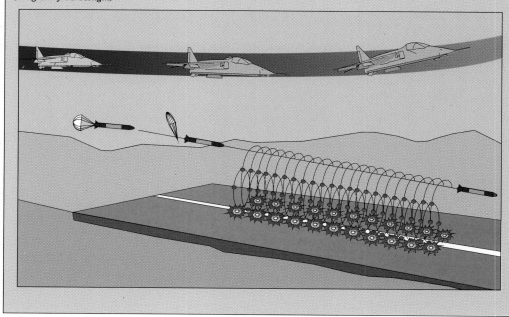

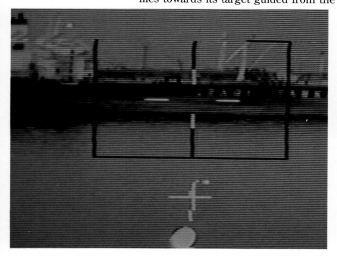

Above:
At break of day a fully loaded Jaguar A of *Escadron* 4/11 *Jura* takes off with bombs for the Iraqi army, a drop-tank for the trip, and AAMs for the unlikely event of an encounter with Saddam's air force.
(Photo: SIRPA-Air)

use against hardened targets. It can be launched from more than six miles' range; and can penetrate more than six feet of hardened concrete. The AS-3OL's high performance was the reason that the US command tasked the French pilots with attacking the major munitions depot in occupied Kuwait.

The AS-30L has a length of just under twelve feet and a diameter of thirteen inches; it weighs about 1,146lbs, compared with the nearly 2,000 lbs. of the US 'Paveway', and this low weight allows the Jaguar to carry two AS-30Ls. Once launched, the missile flies towards its target guided from the Jaguar by means of an axial gyroscope system until the terminal stage, when an internal final guidance system takes it on to the target.

Some 800 have been delivered, including some to Jordan, Egypt, and… Iraq. Saddam had acquired 300 of these weapons, but luckily had expended most of them during his long war with Iran. ❏

Below:
Frames from the camera in the Atlis laser target designation pod used by a Jaguar during the delivery of an AS-30L missile to an Iraqi tanker in the Gulf.
(Photo: SIRPA-Air)

THE ROYAL AIR FORCE

Opposite top:
Checking 'the height of a camel's eye above the ground', one of the Tornado GR.1s from the RAF detachment at Tabuk. *(Photo: MoD/RAF)*

Among the European nations there was least public opposition to sending troops to the Gulf in Great Britain, where anti-war demonstrations were of negligible size. The average British man in the street holds the professional armed forces in high regard, and generally feels supportive towards them, especially if they face active service. The successful Falklands campaign of 1982 is still remembered with pride; and Saddam Hussein's cat-and-mouse game with thousands of British civilian hostages taken in Kuwait aroused national fury. The Royal Air Force sent around 80 combat aircraft to the theatre of war; flew some of the most dangerous missions, from the first hours of 'Desert Storm'; and, with seven Tornados lost, paid proportionately the highest price of any coalition air force.

All the available Tornado GR.1 bombers and F.3 fighters took part in the first wave of attacks on the night of 16/17 January. They took off at 1.50a.m. from their bases at Dhahran and Tabuk in Saudi Arabia and Muharraq in Bahrain, and headed north. Their mission was to bomb Iraqi airfields with their JP-233 runway-attack weapons, and to destroy the radars around these bases with their ALARM missiles.

Opposite below:
Jaguar GR.1 from No.41 (Composite) Sqn. at Muharraq, Bahrain nears the Kuwaiti border en route to bomb a convoy of Iraqi vehicles. *(Photo: MoD/RAF)*

'At a distance of ten miles the dark night was suddenly lit up by intensive anti-aircraft fire', reported a Tornado pilot from No.9 Squadron. Despite this impressive reception the Tornados pressed home their attacks, and returned unscathed. Later on the

Above:
Parked under a basic sun-shelter at Dhahran, this Tornado F.3 of No.11 (Composite) Sqn. is equipped with two drop-tanks and Sky Flash AAMs. *(Photo: Eric Micheletti)*

17th, however, they had to hit the same targets again, to ensure their long-term denial to Saddam's fighters. Again they attacked at very low altitude; and although many of the sophisticated SAM defences had been knocked out, the wall of anti-aircraft cannon fire was undiminished. Coming in at more than 600mph and less than 100 feet, the RAF pilots later claimed to know from experience the exact

height of a camel's eye above the ground…

On the afternoon of 17 January eight RAF Jaguar GR.1s of No.41 (Comp.) Sqn. began hitting supply routes and strategic bridges associated with munitions depots in southern Iraq.

The Tornado missions continued nightly; flying in total radio silence to distant, well-defended targets, the RAF strike crews began to suffer regular

51

TORNADOS OVER THE GULF

During the first weeks of 'Desert Storm' the Tornado was the most intensively used European aircraft type. Despite the high loss rate the Tornado GR.1 proved its unmatched capability as an all-weather fighter-bomber.

Three versions were used in the Gulf. Both the Royal Air Force and the Royal Saudi Air Force employed the GR.1 IDS ('Interdictor Strike') version and the F.3 ADV ('Air Defence Variant'), while only the RAF had the GR.1A reconnaissance version. By 17 January the RAF had about 60 Tornado GR.1s and F.3s in-theatre, and the RSAF, 44; the Italian air force also deployed ten Tornado IDS to Al Dhafra in the United Arab Emirates.

Until 25 January the primary mission of the Tornados, both British and Saudi, was to attack Iraqi military airfields, which proved very well defended by anti-aircraft batteries. Gen. Chuck Horner, commanding the coalition air forces, rated the Tornados as having done an outstanding job, attacking 15 Iraqi bases — a third of the active total. But the inherent risk in attacking at very low altitude against lethal ground fire resulted in the loss of four RAF Tornados in the first four days.

For this kind of mission the Tornados are equipped with JP-233 munitions pods, capable of destroying a runway with its bomblets; and with 1,000-lb. 'iron bombs' and ALARM anti-radar missiles. The Tornado is not, however, equipped with a laser target designator; so a squadron of RAF Buccaneers was sent to the Gulf at the end of January to provide designation for both Tornados and Jaguars.

The last to arrive in the Gulf were three reconnaissance Tornado GR.1As; these are identical to the GR.1 except for having the two cannon replaced by an infra-red system based around the Vinten Linescan 4000. This aircraft also has a video camera giving excellent resolution and allowing 'real time' viewing.

The F.3 interceptors were tasked with covering allied air raids and destroying Iraqi aircraft, operating in conjunction with AWACS. The F.3 carries four Sidewinder AIM-9L and four British Aerospace Sky Flash AAMs. Originally designed to intercept Soviet long-range bombers over Europe, the F.3 lacks combat agility against new-generation light fighters; nevertheless it has excellent endurance, is air-refuellable, and is a potent offensive and defensive fighter.

losses. At the end of the first week of operations, after a total of 600 sorties, five two-man crews were missing in action. Two aircrew were among those paraded on Baghdad TV, and threatened with dispersal as 'human shields' at strategic sites. Wing Commander David Henderson, RAF detachment commander in Bahrain, responded hotly to criticism of his tired but indomitable crews: 'When the details of our operational missions can be revealed, people will understand why we suffered these losses.'

Faced with the loss of virtually an aircraft per raid, however, the RAF took advantage of the increased freedom of Iraqi skies to change tactics, abandoning the ultra-low level attacks. From this point on the anti-runway missions were flown at medium altitude; and the RAF was also tasked with destroying other types of target. Military production sites and storage depots were allocated; and on 27 January six Tornado GR.1s attacked a huge munitions depot in the Basra area with great success. The secondary explosions were colossal, and continued over several days. On the 28th an important refinery in the same area was severely damaged.

Perhaps the most important targets at this stage, however, were the SAM missile sites, especially in Kuwait. These were so comprehensively bombed that they virtually ceased to exist. At the end of the second week of the war a senior RAF staff officer

THE JP-233 ANTI-RUNWAY SYSTEM

This specially-developed podded system for RAF fighter-bombers is used specifically against enemy airfields. It comprises two parts: one half of the pod contains 30 x 50-lb. SG-357 sub-munitions, able to penetrate concrete and create large craters. The other half contains 215 x 4-lb. HB-876 bomblets which, with a variety of fuse settings, increase the damage, prevent its repair, and render runways unusable for a long period. The JP-233 can also be used against high-value tactical targets or vehicle concentrations. Each Tornado GR.1 carries two pods.

(Diagram: J.M. Mongin)

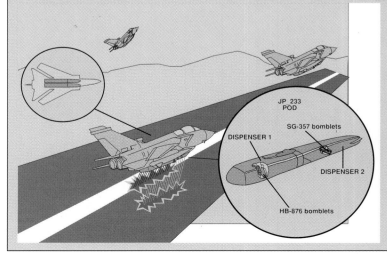

remarked: 'We are in no hurry; we can take our time to select our targets and to destroy them.'

From the second week the RAF was also tasked with seeking out and destroying Scud missile sites. The Tornado GR.1s identified the targets, and the Jaguars attacked them, often running in at less than 100 feet altitude to avoid tracking by any anti-aircraft artillery acquisition radars which might still be operating. High above the battlefield the Tornado F.3 heavy fighters maintained combat air patrols. These missions were of great value; and on 1 February allied intelligence concluded that all Scud launchers and associated vehicles in occupied Kuwait had been destroyed.

Two factors had made the effective contribution of the RAF air crews possible, above all other considerations. The Tornado GR.1's mission, for years past, had been training in Europe for just this kind of hazardous low-level strike deep behind the Iron Curtain; in the normal course of training a certain level of accidental losses had been accepted as inevitable. Secondly, RAF aircraft were deployed to the Gulf region as early as August 1990, and thus their rotated crews had months to familiarise themselves with the desert environment. When the time came to fight, they were able to maintain high states of readiness and to fly missions daily — often, twice daily — in strength. ❏

Above:
Joint mission by RAF Jaguar GR.1 of No.41 Sqn. from Muharraq, carrying a recce pod containing five Vinten F-59 and F-126 cameras; and a Tornado GR.1 of No.31 Sqn. from the same base.
(Photo: Mod/RAF)

Opposite top:
Impressive head-on view of a Tornado fighter equipped with four Sky Flash and two Sidewinder AAMs.
(Photo: MoD/RAF)

Left:
In a hardened shelter, one of the Buccaneers — elderly, but with a vital laser designation capability and massively strong — sent out to the Gulf after the war began to operate with the Tornados.
(Photo: MoD/RAF)

THE WAR OF THE BRIDGES

After attacking Iraqi strategic targets, then the rear-echelon elements of the army massed in Kuwait and around Basra in south-east Iraq, the coalition air forces turned from the first week of February to Saddam's lines of communication and supply. The geography of Iraq made the most effective solution the cutting of all bridges south of Baghdad, which would sever the umbilical between northern and southern armies. While the massive bombardment of the Republican Guard, and the search for Scud launchers, were both pursued, the systematic destruction of bridges over the Euphrates and Tigris Rivers began from 5 February. That night US and British aircraft completely destroyed the large Bridge of the Republic in the heart of Baghdad. Three days later the Bridge of 14 July was destroyed, and the Bridge of Martyrs was seriously damaged (although partially repaired by Iraqi engineers with a temporary structure).

The peak of this campaign came on 10 and 11 February, when more than 80% of the RAF's Tornado/Buccaneer attack teams were targeted on bridges, day and night. RAF Intelligence later calculated that some 24 sorties were required to take out each bridge. Three bridges destroyed at Nasiriyya, 100 miles from Basra and 236 miles from Baghdad, were the crowning prize: they represented a vital choke-point on the supply lines south. In less than two weeks 90% of the Euphrates and Tigris bridges between Baghdad and the Kuwaiti border had been cut; and from 13 February the flow of supplies to the Iraqi army in the south was cut to less than 10% of its volume before 17 January.

One of the Tornado GR.1s of the RAF's No.20 (Composite) Squadron, based at Tabuk, Saudi Arabia, shows off its desert camouflage. These aircraft kept up constant attacks from 17 January. *(Photo: Ian Black)*

INTERDICTOR-STRIKE AIRCRAFT
PANAVIA TORNADO GR.1

Crew: Two
Top speed: 1,370mph
Powerplant: Two Turbo-Union RB.199-34R Mk.101
Basic weight: 14 tons
Loaded weight: 27.2 tons
Length: 54.8 tons
Height: 18.6ft.
Wing span (unswept): 45.5ft.; **(swept):** 28.2ft.
Armament: 2 x 27mm Mauser cannon; for airfield attacks, 2 x JP-233 munitions dispenders, 2 x AIM-9L Sidewinder AAMs, one chaff pod, one Sky Shadow ECM pod

ROYAL AIR FORCE IN THE GULF
(January – February 1991)

Fighters

18 Tornado F.3	No. 43 (Composite) Sqn.	Dhahran

Ground attack aircraft

12 Jaguar GR.1	No. 41 (Composite) Sqn.	Thumrait, Oman, later Muharraq, Bahrain
15 Tornado GR.1	No. 15 (Composite) Sqn.	Muharraq
12 Tornado GR.1	No. 20 (Composite) Sqn.	Tabuk, SA
12 Tornado GR.1	No. 31 (Composite) Sqn.	Muharraq
12 Buccaneer S.2A/S.2B	From Nos. 12 and 208 Sqns.	

Miscellaneous aircraft

11 Chinook HC.1	} Joint Helicopter	
19 Puma HC.1	} Support Unit	} Ras al Ghar, SA

Mixed formation of Tornado GR.1 strike aircraft
and Tornado F.3 fighters over the Gulf.
(Photo: Ian Black)

AIRCRAFT LOSSES IN THE FIRST FEW DAYS

The loss of five aircraft and their crews in the first week (and a sixth shortly thereafter) obliged the RAF to change its tactics; luckily the primary task of crippling the Iraqi air force had by then been accomplished. Equipped for low-altitude missions in Central Europe, its squadrons were also capable of delivering laser-guided weapons, but lacked on-board target designation systems for launching them from medium altitude — medium altitude missions would be suicide in Europe. When circumstances allowed them to cease their very low-level airfield attacks in the face of massive 'triple-A' the Tornados and Jaguars operated at medium altitude alongside Buccaneers, in mixed pairs, the Buccaneer 'illuminating' the target with its ASQ-153 Pave Spike designator and the Tornado or Jaguar launching laser-guided munitions from outside AAA range. Happily, seven of the twelve missing Tornado aircrew returned from captivity in March.

MARITIME INTERDICTION MISSIONS

THE IRAQI NAVY GOES TO THE BOTTOM

By the first week of February, some twenty days after the beginning of the air war, the Iraqi navy had effectively ceased to exist. In all, 72 of the 78 vessels with which the navy began the war had been sunk or severely damaged by the coalition air forces. A 73rd would be sunk subsequently, and the remainder would seek refuge in Iranian ports.

The Royal Air Force played a major part in operations to neutralise the Iraqi naval threat, alongside Royal Navy helicopter crews. The Iraqi warships were small, but could not be dismissed: many were capable of launching Exocet or Otomat SSMs, whose potential — especially against crowded carriers or troop ships — was deadly.

The Iraqi vessels which risked going to sea fell victim to either the fighter-bombers or to the Lynx helicopters embarked on Royal Navy warships, which are armed with Sea Skua anti-shipping missiles. The Lynx crews wreaked havoc, particularly during the final naval encounter near Maradin Island. In this engagement the Iraqis lost some 20 vessels, including several missile-armed patrol craft, corvettes, and two frigates which unwisely left port without air cover. Five of the vessels — including an Assad class corvette and a Polnocny class landing ship — were sunk by the RAF Jaguars from 41 (Composite) Squadron at Muharraq, using the new Canadian CRV-7 rocket-launcher. ❑

Above:
RAF combat air patrol along the Iraqi border by a pair of Tornado F.3s from No.5 (Composite) Sqn. based at Dhahran. The aircrews were subsequently replaced by men from No.11 (Composite), and finally No.43 (Composite) Sqns. The Iraqi air force never gave these air superiority fighters the opportunity to use their muscle.
(Photo: Ian Black)

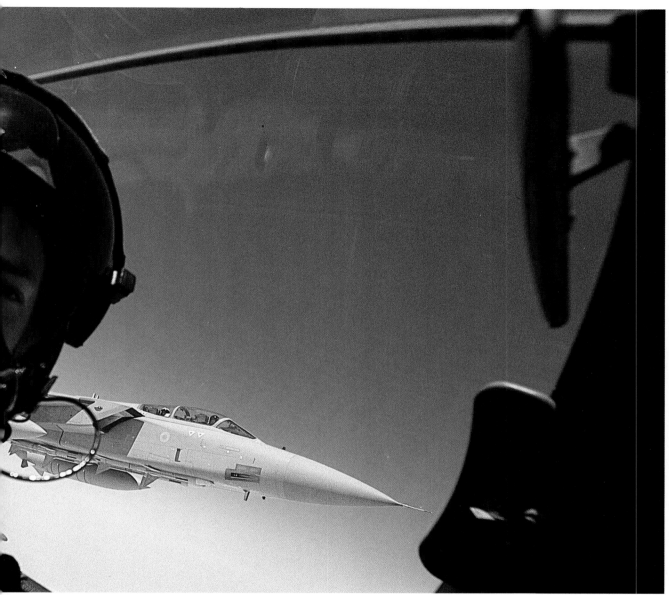

Left:
Tornado F.3 over Arabia, armed with four Sidewinders on the inboard pylons, four Sky Flash semi-recessed under the fuselage, and the underwing drop-tanks more usually seen on the Tornado GR.1.
(Photo: Ian Black)

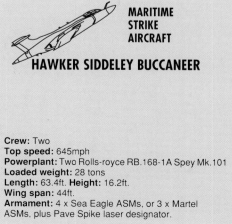

MARITIME STRIKE AIRCRAFT

HAWKER SIDDELEY BUCCANEER

Crew: Two
Top speed: 645mph
Powerplant: Two Rolls-royce RB.168-1A Spey Mk.101
Loaded weight: 28 tons
Length: 63.4ft. **Height:** 16.2ft.
Wing span: 44ft.
Armament: 4 x Sea Eagle ASMs, or 3 x Martel ASMs, plus Pave Spike laser designator.

THE CANADIAN AIR CONTINGENT

Above:
26 Canadian CF-18As of the 439th TFS, 1st Air Division were deployed to Qatar to fly missions with the coalition air forces; their base was guarded by a company of Canadian troops. The Hornets flew several missions in this, the Canadian air force's first shooting war since Korea in 1951.
(Photo: Canadian Armed Forces)

For the first time in 40 years — since the Korean War in 1951 — Canadian military aircraft have taken part in offensive missions.

The first raid against Iraq, which had a greater political than military significance, was launched a week after the start of hostilities. On 24 January, at 7p.m. local time, four CF-18A Hornets of the 439th Tactical Fighter Squadron flew escort for USAF F-16s on a medium altitude bombing mission against Iraqi positions in Kuwait. Just two days earlier the Canadian Parliament in Ottawa had voted unconditional support for United Nations action, authorising the Canadian aircraft based at Doha in Qatar to take part in the coalition's offensive operations.

In all 26 of the Canadian Hornets took part, with 36 pilots. These aircraft were normally based at Baden-Sollingen, Germany, though some of the aircrew were flown out from the base at Cold Lake in Canada, along with a CC-137 tanker. Under the command of Lt. Col. Don Matthews, the Hornets did not carry pylons for offensive weapons; their role was to provide air defence for coalition fighter-bombers with their Sidewinder and Sparrow AAMs.

On 28 January the CF-18As took part in a second night attack as part of a major allied effort. This time it was a real baptism of fire, as Iraqi 'triple-A' opened up on them; but the Canadian fighters suffered no losses, and in fact the greatest danger lay in the sheer number of aircraft in the crowded night sky over the target. As one of the pilots said on his return to base: 'In the middle of the night with your heart pounding, the visual identification of another aircraft looming up at close quarters is kind of exciting...'   ❐

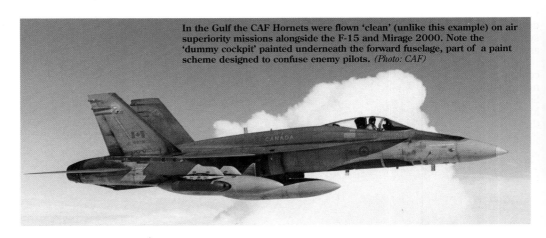

In the Gulf the CAF Hornets were flown 'clean' (unlike this example) on air superiority missions alongside the F-15 and Mirage 2000. Note the 'dummy cockpit' painted underneath the forward fuselage, part of a paint scheme designed to confuse enemy pilots. *(Photo: CAF)*

OPERATION 'LOCUST'

USAF KC-135 tanker. Only one Tornado managed to complete the manoeuvre and pressed on alone — to be shot down by Iraqi anti-aircraft fire over Kuwait. (Happily, the two-man crew were released at the end of the war).

Despite this bad start, two days later, on 20 January, eight Tornados flew another mission against Iraqi positions in southern Kuwait with complete success. On this mission only four aircraft carried bombs, the others being tasked as 'buddy-buddy' refuellers. This tactic was to be the norm for the rest of the Italian air contingent's service in the Gulf.

Thanks to their experience of joint NATO exercises the AMI Tornados were well able to integrate with the other allied air forces. On 12 February they flew as many as 19 missions over Kuwait and Iraq.

On 25 September 1990 eight Panavia Tornado IDS strike aircraft of the *Aeronautica Militare Italiana* — the Italian air force — took off from the base at Bari to deploy to the Gulf. After three weeks of discussion the Italian government had decided to send twelve military aircraft — ten Tornados, a C-130 Hercules and a Fiat G-222 transport — to aid the allied effort. In all, 20 Tornado crews and 270 groundcrew were selected from the 6th *Stormo* at Ghedi, the 36th *Stormo* at Gioia del Colle, and the 50th *Stormo* at Piacenza. For their new deployment the Tornados received new cooling systems for the electronics bays and new sand filters as well as a new paint job.

The C-130 from the 45th *Aerobrigata* which accompanied them to their new base at Al Dhafra, 25 miles north-east of Abu Dhabi, was loaded with Sidewinder and Kormoran missiles, the new German MW-1 dispenser pods, and 27mm ammunition for the Tornado's Mauser cannon. For four months the Italian fighter-bombers trained over the desert.

On the second day of 'Desert Storm', at 2.30a.m., eight Tornados took off for the first Italian air force combat mission since World War II. It was to prove an inauspicious debut. One aircraft had to turn back to base because of technical problems, followed two hours later by six others. In bad weather, they were unable to successfully carry out air refuelling from a

Above:
The eight Italian air force Tornado IDS strike aircraft lined up at Al Dhafra. They used the German MBB MW-1 weapons pod, dispensing sub-munitions equally effective against tanks and 'hardened targets'.
(Photos: Italian Air Force)

Leaving its hardened shelter on the huge Dhahran air base, one of the 12 Tornado F.3s of No.29 Sqn., RSAF. *(Photo: Eric Micheletti)*

Opposite, top:
Tornado F.3 taking off from Dhahran for a long combat air patrol, made possible by the pair of very large drop-tanks. *(Photo: Eric Micheletti)*

Thursday 24 January: and a routine patrol for Captain Ayhed Salah Al-Shamrani of the Royal Saudi Air Force. With his wingman, Capt. Al-Shamrani — an F-15C Eagle pilot of the RSAF's No.42 Squadron based at Dhahran — was ranging high in the blue, about twelve miles inside the Saudi border. Suddenly, a transmission from a patrolling AWACS alerted him: three unidentified aircraft had just crossed the Kuwaiti frontier at low altitude.

A lightning turn, and the two Eagles locked onto the intruders and started their pursuit. At 2,000 yards Al-Shamrani slid in behind his quarry, now clearly visible on radar. 1,500 yards… 900 yards… The intruders were two Iraqi Mirage F-1s (carrying, he later reported, two AM-39 Exocet missiles) and a single MiG-23. The Saudi fighter pilot was armed with two AIM-9L Sidewinder and two AIM-7F Sparrow air-to-air missiles. But he

preferred the Sidewinder for close-in combat, and positioned himself behind the rear Mirage.

The first Sidewinder blazed away, its lock-on tone howling in Al-Shamrani's earphones. The Mirage exploded, the debris cartwheeling down towards the jewel-blue sea. He launched the second; and the second Mirage took a direct hit, apparently oblivious to its danger until the moment it blew up. The allied navies would have nothing to fear from these Exocets. The MiG-23, apparently realising its peril at last, broke off and streaked north. Back at Dhahran Capt. Al-Shamrani — a modest fellow — quickly found himself a national hero, as the first Saudi pilot ever to achieve a 'kill'.

The Royal Saudi Air Force is held in high esteem in the kingdom. It has always been a privileged service, and several princes of the royal family serve as pilots. Prince Bandar, son of Prince Sultan, the Minister of

SIDEWINDERS AND SPARROWS

During the air war only a small number of AIM-9L Sidewinder and AIM-7F Sparrow air-to-air missiles were launched compared with the enormous total of allied missions flown; but those which were launched proved their worth. In total, around 100 AAMs actually left their launch-rails; and these destroyed between 40 and 50 Iraqi aircraft. In 95% of these encounters there was no real combat, more of a 'turkey shoot' — the Iraqi jets chose to turn and run, and thus sealed their fate. The diagram shows the kind of encounter experienced by Capt. Al-Shamrani with an Iraqi Mirage F-1. The F-15C launches its short-range Sidewinder. The missile, guided by infra-red, homes on the heat source produced by the Mirage's engine. Launched at close range, the AIM-9L cannot fail to reach its target: there is no way the quarry can shake it off, or confuse it by launching heat flares. *(Diagram: J. M. Mongin)*.

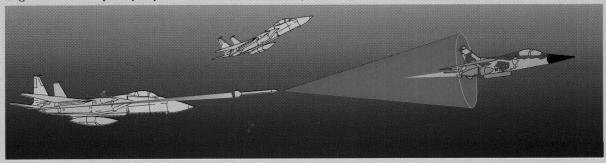

Defence, was sent by his uncle King Fahd to the Royal Air Force's Academy at Cranwell, England, at the tender age of 16. Later he continued his training on F-16s with the United States Air Force. The RSAF is commanded by Prince Khaled, another of the sons of the Minister of Defence.

The RSAF is well equipped for a country with a small population. It has 63 F-15C Eagles, with twelve more on order; 24 Tornado F.3s, 36 Tornado GR.1s, 76 F-5E/Bs, 24 Hawks, and five E-3 AWACS. Trained and advised by the United States and Great Britain, the Saudi pilots are highly competent. The proof is seen in the insignificant losses they suffered during the war: one Tornado, in about 3,000 sorties. The showing made by this fledgling air force in its first war has made the RSAF the pride of the kingdom. ❐

Above & left:
One of the F-15C Eagles of No.13 Sqn., RSAF, also based at Dhahran: detail of the immaculate nose markings, and of technicians working on the avionics bay.
(Photos: Eric Micheletti) 63

A pair of F-15C Eagles of No. 13 Sqn.; this unit had 18 F-15C/Ds on strength, and suffered no losses during the war. Some of the best of all RSAF pilots fly with Nos.13, 5, 6 and 42 fighter squadrons. *(Photo: Yves Debay)*

THE IRAQI AIR BASES

Seven days into the war, the US commanders had to admit that only 17 Iraqi aircraft were confirmed destroyed in air combat, out of a total front-line fleet of some 700. Where were Iraq's combat jets? The answer came from industrial sources in Britain, France, Yugoslavia and other countries. Iraq had eight huge air bases, three of them in the north of the country, built several years ago by European contractors. Typical was the base at Balad in northern Iraq. It had two main runways, an emergency runway, and two taxiways, 4,000 yards long — in all, five usable runways. Each of 45 hardened aircraft shelters (HAS) could protect and operate three or four aircraft.

At least 300 HASs seem to have been built on various Iraqi bases. Each had a roof of two-foot-thick concrete covered by several meters of earth and stones. The main shelter doors, of steel and concrete, were protected by a blast wall of concrete. These made direct air attacks on the doors very difficult during 'Desert Storm', even with laser-guided weapons.

Iraqi engineer teams were trained to effect quick, rough-and-ready repairs to bombed runways. They fired machine guns at any delayed-action ordnance they spotted, cleared damaged areas with bulldozers, and repaired craters with quick-setting concrete. In some cases they had runways usable again in eight hours.

In the event, none of this expense and effort made any difference. The allies' sophisticated 'smart' bombs penetrated many HASs; repeated raids simply cratered repaired runways once more; and the Iraqi air force took off — when it managed to — only to flee to Iran for refuge. By the end of the war some 140 Iraqi aircraft were confirmed lost; and the number of occasions when they made any vain attempt to interfere with allied operations could be counted on the fingers.

Below:
The maintenance of the RSAF's 24 Tornado F.3s is undertaken by British technicians on contract, while their Saudi counterparts are still undergoing training in Britain; the type was only recently introduced to RSAF service. *(Photo: Eric Micheletti)*

RESCUE

القوات الجوية الملكية السعودية
ROYAL SAUDI AIR FORCE

ARMAMENT

THE EMIRATES

One of the Mirage F-1Es of the Qatari Air Force. These aircraft undertook tactical bombing missions over Kuwait from the second week of the war. *(Photo: Dassault Aviation)*
Right:
Line-up of Kuwaiti A-4 Skyhawks at Dhahran. 24 of this type managed to flee the Iraqi invasion, and joined the SAF in 'Free Kuwait' markings. *(Photo: Ian Black)*
Below:
Seen during a pre-delivery test flight, ne of the brand-new Mirage F-1CK and BK of the Kuwaiti Air Force. Based in audi Arabia and maintained by French technicians, they took part in the massive raids of 24 January. *(Photo: Dassault Aviation)*

Acknowledgements:
The author wishes to record his gratitude, for their assistance during the preparation of this book, to: above all, Yves Debay, for the use of his photographs; Jean-Marie Mongin for his diagram designs; Messrs. Houssais, Senior and Junior, for their background knowledge of USAF organisation and access to their insignia collection; the Royal Air Force public information officers of the Ministry of Defence, London; the officers of the parallel department in the US Department of Defense, Washington; Capt. Lefrançois of the public affairs department of the Canadian Armed Forces/Défense Nationale Canadienne; and the officers of SIRPA-Air, in particular Capt. Désir, and Adjudant-Chef Gauthier of the Armée de l'Air.

© 1991 Eric Micheletti

Printed in Singapore

This edition published in Great Britain 1991 by Windrow & Greene Ltd.
5 Gerrard Street, London W1V 7LJ

British Library Cataloguing in Publication Data
Micheletti, Eric
    Air War over the Gulf. (Europa Militaria, v.8)
    1. Middle East. Wars. Air operations.
    I. Title   II. Series
    954.6

ISBN 1-872004-21-0